TRANSITIONAL
ASTROLOGY

TRANSITIONAL ASTROLOGY

GIVING AN ESOTERIC ROLE TO ORTHODOX ASTROLOGY

SUZANNE ROUGH

authorHOUSE®

AuthorHouse™ UK Ltd.
1663 Liberty Drive
Bloomington, IN 47403 USA
www.authorhouse.co.uk
Phone: 0800.197.4150

Published by AuthorHouse 06/05/2014

ISBN: 978-1-4969-8186-8 (sc)
ISBN: 978-1-4969-8187-5 (e)

Library of Congress Control Number: 2014909779

Other Astrological Works by Suzanne Rough

Understanding the Natal Chart: An Esoteric Approach to Learning Horoscopy
Working with Time
Understanding Relationship: Synastry and Compository

Acknowledgments

This work would not have been possible without the commitment of The Lucis Trust to keep the Ageless Wisdom alive. It is dedicated to my mother, Marjorie Rough, who supported me always, even when my path took me where she could not follow

Contents

Preface

This work was written in a twelve-year period during which I was tutored by Master Djwhal Khul (D.K.).

The experience did not make me a Theosophist, because the time of Theosophy had already passed, but it gave me a profound respect for its conceptual structure.

By the time that these tutoring sessions commenced, I had been a full-time professional astrologer for five years, so I was aware of the questions clients bring to astrologers. And they are not, I discovered, the questions they would take to a psychologist.

The questions that bring people to astrologers are mostly about the way forward, about purpose, and about the larger context, which gives a point to our own lives. I was not surprised by this. They had been my questions, too, and those questions had motivated me to become a student of astrology.

We talked of many things relating to astrology in our sessions, but always retuned to *Esoteric Astrology,* the work D.K. had written through Alice Bailey, which first appeared in 1951.

In writing this work, I wanted to create a frame through which I could share with clients and students the insights D.K. shared with me, as well as provide a structure through which practitioners could pass the knowledge on to their own clients and make *Esoteric Astrology* more accessible to the contemporary mind.

Transitional Astrology was first made available as a teaching manual in 2000. I have made a few revisions for the purposes of this edition to reflect the changes that have taken place in the spiritual seekers' world since then. Mostly, the revisions involve removing comments that pertained to developments in New Age teaching at the close of the previous century. That era is now over, and we spiritual seekers, in the way we use our lives and time, will have to discover for ourselves whether we are the poorer or freer for that.

Suzanne Rough
March 2014

Introduction

Thank you for your interest in this work.

Coming to grips with this approach to astrology will take determination and application, but you will hopefully be rewarded by a different understanding of the system in which we live, move, and have our being and a different perspective on self and upon what can be done with the opportunity that is our lifetime. This understanding may then be passed on to your own clients, pupils, those with whom you might discuss these matters in everyday life, and those who observe the way you organise your own life.

Our purpose in offering the course is to make a contribution toward getting into circulation and usage the knowledge that through his amanuensis, Alice Bailey, the Master Djwhal Khul made available to humanity.

Alice Bailey's *Esoteric Astrology,* published by the Lucis Press in 1951, is the standard text in this field, and we draw heavily upon this work in Part 1, taking care to define and explain the concepts in a way which will make them more accessible to the contemporary mind. This is done with Master D.K.'s expressed consent and approval.

Esoteric Astrology appeared in a different time and cultural environment from that in which we live today.

Later in the work, we will address the matter of building of a bridge between the ideas laid out in Part 1 and everyday life. It is the way of esotericism to move from the general to the particular.

Those of you who have already tried to penetrate *Esoteric Astrology* will know that it is not an easy read. Indeed, it was never designed to be. The denseness of the text and the many obscurities are put into place to prevent the knowledge falling into the hands of those who are not yet ready for the ideas.

The obscurities are not riddles. Many do not yield their secret even after close and careful examination. Indeed, a closer examination sometimes reveals that the smoke screen is thicker than it at first appeared. This is particularly true in respect to the solar systems. Master D.K. insists that these safeguards must stay in place. His explanation is interesting: The solar systems—the phenomenal expression of the second divine aspect—contain the matrix for the unfolding of consciousness and wide-scale misunderstanding and wrong thinking that could adversely affect this unfoldment.

Despite its difficulties, *Esoteric Astrology* is a rewarding read. For an astrologer, it is a lifetime's education condensed into one volume. Do, please, have a go at it if you have not already. It is widely distributed in a range of languages. On the matter of reading the Alice Bailey material, D.K. has said that he recommends twenty minutes of quality reading in one sitting. After this time, the brain will get too tired to take in much more.

Every good wish as you commence upon this work. There are sure to be times when you think you understand less than you did when you started out, but there will be other times when you will feel inspired by what you have learned. That is the way of the learning process when the mind has to struggle with unfamiliar concepts. We all have to tread this path and endure the discomforts if we want the benefits of the knowledge. There is no other route. Persistence pays! Throughout this work, I reference *Estoeric Astrology* the publication and esoteric astrology the branch of astrology to which it has made such a crucial contribution.

Recommended Reading

Reference is made in the course of the chapters to certain works that may be of interest in enlarging understanding in specific areas.

Essential works of reference for anyone studying transitional astrology are:
- *Esoteric Astrology,* Alice Bailey, Lucis Trust, 1951.
- *Ponder On This,* Lucis Trust, 1971. Excellent for bringing clarity to key terms and ideas.
- *The Masters and the Path,* C.W. Leadbeater, Theosophical Publishing House, 1925. Showing its age stylistically, but unsurpassed in its delineation of the work of the hierarchy and the hierarchy's requirements of disciples.
- *The Secret Doctrine,* Theosophical Publishing Company, Limited,1888, H.P. Blavatsky. Although it is not recommended for those starting out, honourable mention must be made to the founding work of Theosophy that still has secrets to yield when we are ready to receive them.

Suzanne Rough
March 2000

Part One

The Context

> "All the energies—zodiacal, systemic, and planetary—have a definite effect upon all the lives in all the forms of all the kingdoms of nature. Nothing can escape these radiatory and magnetic influences. The goal for the evolution of humanity is to become consciously and livingly aware of the nature of these energies and to begin to know them and use them. This is the field of occultism as the hierarchy has always told men."
> *Esoteric Astrology*

The aim of this chapter is to provide a context for the practice of horoscopy. We are not, to use Master D.K's expression, "factors of isolated importance," but rather, participants in a stupendous process of unfolding consciousness.

"I was a treasure unknown, and I longed to be known. Then I created a creation to which I made myself known; then they knew me." So runs one of the most well-known of Islam's non-canonical Hadiths.

Our universe is the result of that longing, and we are a part of that process of unfolding consciousness and knowing.

Traditionally, conventional astrology has not been unconcerned with the larger picture. Esoteric astrology, the subject of which is the development of consciousness, must be more inclusive because becoming conscious is a process of developing inclusiveness. If you do not find it easy to take in the information in this chapter, be patient with yourself. Be prepared, if necessary, to give yourself many runs at it, and draw up your own diagrams to assist the assimilation of the information.

Certain minds can absorb this kind of information far more readily than others. And again, some of the statements made in this chapter will require the construction of a context for their significance to become apparent. It is context that turns knowledge into understanding.

The construction of a context can be a slow (and some would say) unending task.

The chapters that follow will have a more obvious, immediate, and practical relevance to the practice of astrology. It is important to take away from this section at least an awareness that the field of space is a web of moving energies; an awareness that we all belong to a great living, breathing universe; and an awareness of three, seven, and twelve as numerical groupings of significance.

Of the twelve, the five serve the seven; of the seven, the four serve the three; and the three are aspects of the one.

Definitions

Term used with frequency in this module	Definition	Parallel term from *'Esoteric Astrology'*
World	Cosmos; dimension.	Logos; Being
Cosmic	Belonging to the constellations, i.e. beyond our solar system.	
Systemic	Belonging to our solar system.	
The major constellations	The Great Bear; Sirius; the Pleiades.	The Intimate Constellations
Ray	Representative of one of the seven solar systems, of which our system is one.	An expression of a solar life
Zodiacal constellations	The 12 constellations of the Milky Way which comprise our zodiac.	Stupendous and Unfathomable Lives
Creative Hierarchy	Level of being of which there are twelve in total in the life of the present solar system. Five are out of manifestation and are active on the Cosmic Astral plane, and seven are in manifestation. Of the seven, four are in etheric matter only and three in dense physical matter.	State of Being
Planetary i)	Belonging to the planets.	Great Entities
ii)	The spiritual natures of the planetary Logoi, seven in total and found in etheric matter upon the second plane of our solar system.	Heavenly Men;
Sacred planet	Having taken five cosmic initiations. The awareness of the Logos of a sacred planet transcends the knowledge and awareness of our solar system and is responsive to the life of	

	Sirius and, to a degree, to that of the Pleiades also.	
Non-sacred planet	Having taken three cosmic initiations. The Logos of a non-sacred planet is becoming inclusive in his consciousness to all that is found within our solar system and is becoming responsive to the life of Sirius.	
Atom	In the context of this lesson: a separate unit from one of the kingdoms of nature.	
Family	One of four categories of organic life. The fifth kingdom, the Kingdom of Souls, emerges from the Fourth, the human kingdom.	Family/kingdom
Force	Focused energy; it is consciousness which provides the focus.	
Ensoul	The process whereby a conscious entity takes on a body of lower vibrational matter.	
Involutionary	Pertaining to the form building aspect of life i.e. the descent into matter.	
Initiation	Attainment of a higher level of consciousness.	A process of developing inclusiveness
Chakra	Energy centre in the etheric vehicle of a being.	Centre

Diagram 1

World			Life span *	breath *
Protocosmos Absolute 1			9.10^{28} yrs	9.10^{19} yrs
All starry worlds 2			3.10^{24} yrs	3.10^{15} yrs
Suns and Milky Way 3		*future*	9.10^{19} yrs	90 bill yrs
Deuterocosmos Our Sun 1 4			3.10^{15} yrs	3 mill yrs
Planets 2 5		*present*	90 bill yrs	80 yrs
Tritocosmos Life on Earth *1* 3 6			3 mill yrs	24 hrs
Bodies *2* 4 7			80 yrs	3 secs
Large cells 3 5			24 hrs	0.0001sec
Small cells *4* 6		*past*	3 secs	unknown
Molecule 5 7			0.0001 sec	unknown
Electrons 6			0.000000003 sec	unknown
Protons 7			unknown	unknown

*Calculated by P.D. Ouspensky.

Diagram 2

The Expression of the Second Aspect

	Human	Planetary Logos	Our Solar Logos	The Solar Logos
Spiritual expression	The Heart centre in the Head	Sirius	Central Spiritual Sun (Second Aspect); identity undisclosed	Central spiritual Sun (First Aspect); identity undisclosed
Soul expression	The egoic body	The Heavenly Men	Sirius	undisclosed
Physical expression	The heart centre	The Hierarchy	The Heavenly Men	Sirius

Chapter 1

The Seven Worlds

"All knowledge starts with Cosmoses."—G.I. Gurdjieff

"Study of the world, study of the universe is based on the study of some fundamental laws which are not generally known or recognised in science. The two chief laws are the law of three and the law of seven."—P.D. Ouspensky

The Structure of the Universe

The Worlds

We inhabit a universe composed of seven dimensions. We will call them worlds. Each of these worlds is a living, breathing, conscious, evolving entity, each contained by or containing the other worlds and coexistent with them. Collectively, they span three planes of consciousness: the cosmic mental, the cosmic astral, and the cosmic physical.

Down the ages and across the many spiritual traditions, these worlds have been called by many different names. We will simply number them one to seven.

Collectively and with the rest of organic life on earth, humanity belongs to World Six. Individually, we each belong to World Seven, the world of the atom. Each of us is an atom of the human family, a separate unit, just as each cat, dog, and tree is an atom of its respective family. Our world, World Seven, has been called, inelegantly but usefully, the world of bodies. A more familiar name is the microcosm.

The seven worlds represent a period of dimensions. Although there are more worlds (ie, the microscopic worlds of cells, molecules, and electrons), time being different in each of the worlds, there are only ever seven dimensions existing for each other. The lives in the smaller worlds are over before the larger worlds have had the time to register an impression of them, in which case they are always the past in relation to these larger worlds (see Endnote 1). Of the microscopic worlds, we will simply say, and as a point of interest, our bodies (World Seven) are to the molecule what the sun (World Four) is to us.

World	Identity	Body of manifestation	Comments
One	Absolute Monad 'The One of Whom Naught can be said' *Esoteric Astrology*	The Universe	The Cause of all that is.
Two	The Solar Logos* 'The One Greater than our Logos' *Esoteric Astrology*	The starry worlds/ all galaxies	Manifests the quality of the Absolute Monad. The Solar Logos is a sevenfold Being. Three constellations from this world are of particular importance to us: the Great Bear; Sirius; the Pleiades. They are energy centres in the body of the Being. This is the world in which the Seven Rays can be said to originate.
Three		The Suns of the Milky Way/ our galaxy	Contains the twelve zodiacal constellations.
Four	'Our' Solar Logos	Our solar system	Our solar system constitutes one aspect of this sevenfold Being, the Solar Logos, which with the planets, creates a unit which may be described as 'our' Solar Logos.
Five		The planets	Comprising seven sacred planets; five non-sacred planets; and approximately 70 'hidden' planets i.e. existing in etheric matter only.
Six	The Planetary Logos	Our planet Earth	Organic life on earth comprising four

			kingdoms: • the mineral kingdom - *first* • the vegetable kingdom - *second* • the animal kingdom - *third* • the human kingdom - *fourth* • out of which evolves the Kingdom of Souls - *fifth*
Seven		Atoms/bodies	The separate beings from all the species in World Six.

* In *Esoteric Astrology,* the term "Solar Logos" usually refers to "our" Solar Logos whose relationship to the other aspects of this sevenfold being is not disclosed, but the matter is not always made clear.

Plane of consciousness	Composition	Consciously active on all seven sub-planes
Cosmic Mental	7 sub-planes: 4 higher 3 lower	Absolute Monad
Cosmic Astral	7 sub-planes: 4 higher 3 lower	The Solar Logos
Cosmic Physical	7 sub- planes: • etheric: 4 • dense physical: 3 •	'Our' solar Logos

The planes of the cosmic physical plane are logoic, monadic, atmic, buddhic, mental (upper and lower), astral (upper and lower), and physical (etheric and dense physical).

All the beings of all the worlds are struggling to achieve their goals, which are different in detail, but common in that they involve the accessing of a higher level of consciousness.

- The goal of the Solar Logos is to include consciousness of the higher cosmic mental planes.
- The goal of "our" Solar Logos is to include consciousness of the higher cosmic astral planes.
- The goal of the sacred planets is to achieve consciousness of the lower cosmic astral planes.
- The goal of the non-sacred planets is to achieve consciousness of the seven planes of our solar system.

♦ The goal of the human kingdom is to include consciousness of the higher mental plane of our solar system.

The seven worlds are a ladder upon which those on the higher rungs help the lower and are in turn helped by the efforts of the lower. For one world to rise, all worlds must rise.

The Triads

"When three forces meet together, things happen. If they do not come together, nothing happens."—P.D. Ouspensky

First Divine Aspect: **Life** *Active*	Life is what animates and sustains
Second Divine Aspect: **Quality** *Passive*	Quality is the consciousness of a being
Third Divine Aspect: **Appearance** *Neutralizing*	Appearance in form manifests the quality of a being

Throughout the universe, this threefold division is in evidence. There are other significant divisions of the unity that is the absolute, but we will start with the threefold division.
Every being within the universe encompasses these three aspects, and the universe itself has manifested because the first (active) and second (passive) aspects have made contact through the third (neutralising) aspect.

This creates a triad, and as can be seen from studying the passage of force in the universe (below), the third and neutralising aspect within the triad becomes the first and active principle in a triad forming on a lower level.

The first triad: The Trinity
First aspect: God the Father
Second aspect: God the Son
Third aspect: God the Holy Spirit

Triads are of considerable importance in *Esoteric Astrology*. Three is the number of spirit.

The Passage of Forces in the Universe

Force from the Absolute Monad is distributed through the worlds, with each of the other worlds acting as both recipient and transmitter. Space is etheric in nature, and the ethers enable transmission. It is described by those with etheric sight as a network of moving, golden light.

It is very important to the understanding of the rays in particular that the flow of force through the universe is understood. The active principle in any triad distributes, not to the world directly below it, but to the next world down. This world then returns it to the world above it, which sends it back, transformed, to the lower world, which then sends it on to the next-but-one world.

The movement therefore describes a loop effect. Consciousness is the medium for the return of energies within a human being and throughout all the worlds of the universe.

The first triad:
The Trinity = World One

The second triad:
World One distributes to World Three. World Three
sends this energy to World Two, which then returns it, transformed, to World Three.

The third triad:
World Three distributes to World Five. World Five sends this energy to
World Four, which then returns it, transformed, to World Five.

The fourth triad:
In this triad, the distributions arrangement undergoes change.
World Five distributes to World Seven. World Seven sends the energy into the environment, World Six, via the health aura of each living member. These worlds do not distribute to lower worlds, but when any organism dies, the etheric matter released goes to the moon.

The moon, which is a satellite of the Earth and not, in its own right, a member of World Five, is involved in the creation of a fifth, and from the standpoint of human consciousness, an involutionary triad, involving Worlds Six and Seven and the physical body of the Earth.

The challenge for humanity is to withhold from the moon and to create, via the mental plane and the causal body, a bridge to World Five. This can be done only by the conscious activity of the living organism. This is the raison d'être of spiritual activity in the human kingdom. The other kingdoms that make up World Six do not have this capacity. This creates an alternative scenario within the fourth triad: A conscious man in World Seven returns the energy to World Five.

The Transforming Centres

Triad	Identity	Transforming centre/ body of manifestation	Plane of consciousness on which transformation takes place
The second	The Solar Logos	The starry worlds	Cosmic Astral
The third	'Our' Solar Logos	The solar system	Cosmic Physical
The fourth	the Planetary Logos	Life on earth Conscious man	i) Dense physical ii) Higher mental

There are three transforming centres in the universe, four if humanity produces conscious men. We will see as we go on to study the second numerical grouping of importance, the seven, that the fourth principle permits a process to continue beyond the original triad.

This should indicate something of the importance of the role of the human kingdom in the development of consciousness in the lower kingdoms of nature and in the subatomic worlds, which for us are the past. This involves the process we call redemption.

The Major Constellations

The major constellations are as follows:

- ♦ The Great Bear, the stars of which are the seven head centres and the representatives of the first aspect of the "One Greater than our Logos."
- ♦ Sirius, the heart centre of this great being, represents the second aspect. It should be noted that Sirius is a sun. Suns are the medium of expression for the second aspect.
- ♦ The Pleiades represent the third aspect and comprise the throat centre.

All three major constellations are involved in the transmission of the seven rays to World Three.

The Seven Rays

The second grouping of importance to us is the seven. So far, we have identified the seven worlds and the seven planes of the consciousness. Within the seven, there is always the dominant three, the interceding fourth, and the subsidiary three.

The interceding fourth and the subsidiary three enable the continuation of the flow of force beyond the originating triad. This is under law (see Endnote 2). If we look back to the beginning of the chapter and to the seven worlds, we can identify the major three which form the first triad (worlds one, two, and three); the interceding fourth (World Four: our solar system), and the subsidiary three (Worlds Fve, Six, and Seven).

The seven planes of consciousness also conform to this structure.

When the process is reversed and energy is returned from lower to higher (the path of return), the role of the fourth principle is to transform and redeem. The number seven represents the emergence of consciousness out of matter. It is the number of soul.

We meet the seven again in the form of the seven cosmic rays of the seven solar systems that ensoul them.

The seven rays are the product of the force from the Absolute Monad working on the substance of World Three, which is then returned to World Two. This energy is then transformed and returned, in the form of the seven rays, to World Three via the three major constellations.

The rays originate therefore on the second plane of the universe, the cosmic astral plane. They are agents of the second divine aspect, and they reflect the sevenfold nature of the Solar Logos, "The One Greater than our Logos," who expresses the second principle and expresses the quality of God.

The rays express seven principles of spiritual will: first (initiating), second (understanding), third (structuring, knowing), fourth (synthesising, redeeming), fifth (liberating), sixth (submitting), and seventh (fusing).

The rays are distributed by the suns and constellations of World Three. Our system ensouls one of the cosmic rays and the subrays of the remaining six rays.

When emanating from the Great Bear, the seven rays are agents of active force to the planetary world. From the Pleiades, they are the agents of passive force. The substance of our solar system provides the third, neutralising force.

Each of the rays entering our solar system is the recipient and custodian of energies coming from the seven solar systems (of which ours is one) and the twelve constellations.

Each is actuated by three streams of force:
- systems other than our own
- our own solar system
- our own planetary life

Each ray expresses an energy principle and manifests its quality in time and space. It is that quality that determines its phenomenal appearance. This is expressed through the creative hierarchies. The major rays are the first, second, and third, while the minor rays are the fourth, fifth, sixth, and seventh.

All the minor rays are rays of attribute of the major third ray.
- The fourth synthesises the fifth, sixth, and seventh and acts as the intercessor between the major three and the subsidiary three.
- The fifth ray is a differentiation of the third.
- The sixth ray is a differentiation of the second.
- The seventh ray is a differentiation of the first.

Ray	Description	Colour	Principle
Ray I	Will to Power	Orange	Initiating *1st*
Ray II	Love-Wisdom	Blue	Understanding, developing consciousness *2nd*
Ray III	Active Intelligence	Green	Knowing (through form and structure) *3rd*
Ray IV	Harmony through Conflict	Yellow	Synthesizing, interceding *4th*
Ray V	Concrete Science	Indigo	Liberating (spirit from matter via the mental plane) *5th*
Ray VI	Devotion	Red	Submitting (to an ideal) *6th*
Ray VII	Ceremonial Magic	Violet	Fusing (spirit and matter) *7th*

The Zodiacal Constellations

There are twelve zodiacal constellations. Twelve is the third grouping of significance to us. Within the twelve, the five serve the seven, as the past serves the present.
The number twelve represents experience within form. It is the number of the personality.

The twelve zodiacal constellations, unlike the major constellations, may belong to our galaxy, but D.K. describes them as unfathomable. They contain within them the six solar systems that are companions to our own, and collectively, they represent the third divine aspect.

What little human consciousness can grasp about their influence in our solar system is collected together under the twelve zodiacal signs (see Endnote 3).

The twelve constellations distribute to the planets, which then return this force to the sun for transformation.

Each ray enters our solar system by means of three constellations because the lives that express these rays embody within themselves the three aspects.

Ray	First Aspect	Second Aspect	Third Aspect
Ray I	Aries	Leo	Capricorn
Ray II	Gemini	Virgo	Pisces
Ray III	Cancer	Libra	Capricorn
Ray IV	Taurus	Scorpio	Sagittarius
Ray V	Leo	Sagittarius	Aquarius
Ray VI	Virgo	Sagittarius	Pisces
Ray VII	Aries	Cancer	Capricorn

All the rays enter our solar system, although not all three aspects of all seven rays are expressed within them. Within our system, the rays are distributed by the planets (see Chapter 2).

Endnotes:

1. The Seven Worlds

The seven worlds that coexist for each other comprise two groupings of three. Both of the groupings contain worlds that are contemporaneous with each other but not with three worlds comprising the other group. The link is provided by the fourth world is common to both and provides a bridge in time.

2. The Law of Seven

Much could be said about this law and its effects, which is summarised by Ouspensky thusly, "It means that no process in the world goes without interruptions."
For the purposes of this work, we will confine ourselves to emphasising the importance of the interceding fourth.
Without this intercession, there could be no descent beyond the originating triad. On the path of return, which is our concern as esoteric astrologers, the interceding fourth has to act as the bridge between the higher and the lower.

Interceding fourths of significance to our study are:
- ♦ our solar system
- ♦ Earth
- ♦ humanity
- ♦ the ego
- ♦ the heart

Strongly recommended as further reading is Ouspensky's *In Search of the Miraculous,* published by Routledge and Kegan Paul 1950. Ouspensky was a scientist, working with the third and fifth rays. Born and educated in Russia, he was from a very different culture from that which embraced Theosophy. To the unprepared reader, Ouspensky's books may seem both chilly and doomy. As occult works, however, they are among the finest and most informative in print.

3. *The Zodiac*

Most well-trained astrologers working with orthodox astrology are aware that both the sidereal zodiac used in the Hindu tradition and the tropical zodiac used in Western astrology, are artifices. The division of the path of the sun, itself an illusion, into twelve zones of thirty degrees each, is a framework superimposed upon the belt of stars which is the Milky Way, the constellations of which give their names to the zodiacal signs. The zodiac is a conceptual apparatus which enables us to understand the quality of that force as it is experienced within the system by humanity. It plays no part in the transmission of the force of World Three into our system. That is brought about by the interaction of the constellations and the planets.

Esoteric astrology, like orthodox astrology, supports, for the time being at least, the continued use of the artificial zodiacs.

According to D.K., the zodiacal signs were admitted onto the mental plane in the Atlantean period, and the understanding of the signs which has developed since that time represents the effort of an evolving humanity to comprehend the influence of World Three in our solar system. It is necessarily partial and imperfect, as the lower cannot fully comprehend the higher, but it contains much that is of value to humanity in the tasks of understanding energy and developing consciousness.

Chapter 2

Our Solar System

"Consciousness is dependent upon its vehicle for expression, and both are dependent upon life and energy for existence."—*Esoteric Astrology*

The suns represent transformation and consciousness. They are the intermediary between spirit and matter. They are soul, and their number is seven.

The Solar Logos

Entity manifesting: The Solar Logos
Body of manifestation: The solar system
Receptive centre: Pole of the central sun
Surface radiation or emanation: Solar prana
Movement produced: Systemic rotation
Distributive effect: Solar etheric radiation (felt cosmically)
The Secret Doctrine

First aspect: The central spiritual sun—cosmic mental
plane; body of manifestation: undisclosed.
Second aspect: The heart of the sun—cosmic astral plane; body of manifestation: Sirius.
Third aspect: The physical sun—cosmic physical plane; body of manifestation: the
seven solar systems.

We established in the previous chapter that the Solar Logos is the highest representative of the second aspect. The major constellations represent major chakras in His Body, and His goal is the attainment of the consciousness of the higher cosmic mental planes.

The seven rays are the product of His transformative activity and these He distributes to the lower worlds by means of the seven solar systems, of which ours is one, and the zodiacal constellations.

The seven solar systems may be said to represent His sevenfold personality.

Of the other systems, little is known, but they each ensoul a major cosmic ray and are linked to our own system through the subrays that are distributed into our system by means of the major and zodiacal constellations.

The signs Taurus and Scorpio and the planet Mars are particularly significant in the representation within our solar system of the other systems. This relationship, we are told, is concerned with transforming desire into spiritual will. Its contribution in our system is magnetic energy.

This matter, however, remains a closely guarded secret. The details, D.K. tells us, are disclosed only to initiates of the fifth degree. Equally closely guarded is the secret of the body of manifestation of the central sun, which is the monad to "our" Solar Logos. The star Alcyone, in the Pleiades, around which our solar system is said to orbit, is only a part, or rather, one aspect, of the truth.

"Our" Solar Logos

First aspect: The central spiritual sun—cosmic mental plane
Second aspect: Cosmic astral plane—body of manifestation: Sirius
Third aspect: Cosmic physical plane—body of manifestation: our solar system

"Our" Solar Logos has a second ray soul and a third ray personality.

Our solar system, which manifests the personality, is on the cosmic physical plane; on its seven planes (ie, the subplanes of the cosmic physical plane), the seven rays express themselves in the form of the creative hierarchies, the orders of manifested beings (states of being D.K.) that comprise our solar system in this, its second incarnation.

Our solar system has had a previous incarnation in which manas, the evolution of intelligence, was the goal. It was, we are told, a very material and intellectual incarnation. The goal of the present incarnation is the development of consciousness.

We are also told in *The Secret Doctrine* that the solar system is to Sirius what the human personality is to the ego.

The Creative Hierarchies

The seven creative hierarchies, or ranks of beings, involved in this incarnation are all:
- part of the personality of "our" Solar Logos
- mediators between matter and spirit
- transmitters of force from sources extraneous to the solar system to forms within the solar system
- working under the law of attraction, which is the law of the builders
- interrelated, interacting, and are negative or positive to each other as the case may be

There are twelve creative hierarchies in being, but five are active on the cosmic astral plane and are non-manifesting. This is why the first hierarchy in the following table is numbered six. It is the first of the manifesting hierarchies, but not the first hierarchy.

It is emphasised that the chart below is drawn up with reference only to the human and not to any other kingdom in nature. With reference to the numbering used in the tables, an additional word of explanation is required: the Roman numerals give the rank in a descending order whereas the Arabic numerals give their order from the bottom upwards. The two numbering systems are required so that the Hierarchies and planes of nature may be ranked, according to context, from an involutionary (descending) and evolutionary (ascending) perspective.

The Seven Manifesting Hierarchies

Name / number of Creative Hierachy given in *Esoteric Astrology*	Ray / zodiacal sign with which associated	Plane of Nature	Element	Comments
Divine Flames VI 7	I / Leo	Logoic	Fire - Air	Endeavouring to express the Mental nature of the Solar Logos *World Four*
Divine Builders VII 6	II / Virgo	Monadic	Ether	Endeavouring to express the Astral nature of the Solar Logos: the prototypes of the human monads, 'The Heavenly Men' *Esoteric Astrology Worlds Four & Five*
VII 5	III / Libra	Atmic	Water	Endeavouring to express the Form nature of the Solar Logos *Worlds Four & Five*
Human Hierarchy IX 4	IV / Scorpio	Buddhic	Synthesizing all elements	The human monads *World Five*
Human personality X 3	V / Capricorn	Mental	Fire	The Ego *Worlds Six & Seven*
The Lunar Lords XI 2	VI / Sagittarius	Astral	Water	*Worlds Six & Seven*
Elemental Lives XII 1	VII / Aquarius	Physical	Earth	*World Seven*

The Five Hierarchies Out of Manifestation

Ray/ Zodiacal Sign with which associated	Number down	Number up	Plane
III / Pisces	I	12	Cosmic Astral
IV/ Aries	II	11	Cosmic Astral
V / Taurus	III	10	Cosmic Astral
VI / Gemini	IV	9	Cosmic Astral
VII / Cancer	V	8	on the verge of liberation onto the Cosmic Astral

The seven manifesting hierarchies plus the five out of manifestation total, of course, twelve: the number of experience in form.

The five hierarchies that achieved liberation in the first solar system are serving the seven by sending back their influence by means of the creative hierarchy V, which is on the verge of liberation. The fifth principle (liberation via the mental plane) is involved here, and this hierarchy communicates via the intellectual plane to the fifth hierarchy in manifestation (ie, the human personality).

The Anatomy of "Our" Solar Logos

Collectively, the seven hierarchies of vital lives are the substratum or substance of all that is. This enables us to construct the anatomy of "our" Solar Logos at this stage in His development. As D.K. states, the omissions reveal that "He has yet much to gain cosmically."

Ray	First Aspect	manifesting through	Second Aspect	manifesting through	Third Aspect	manifesting through
I	-	-	*	Divine Flames	*	Human Personality
II	-	-	*	Divine Builders	-	
III	-	-	*	Lesser Builders	*	Human Personality
IV	-	-	*	Human Hierarchy	*	Lunar Lords
V	*	Divine Flames	-	-	*	Human Personality
VI	*	Divine Builders	*	Lunar Lords	-	-
VII	-	-	-	-	*	Human Personality

* denotes manifesting

- denotes absent

Within the body of "Our" Solar Logos: A synoptic view

Creative Hierarchy/ *plane of solar system*	Consciousness of the Logos of a sacred Planet	Consciousness of a perfected man	Consciousness of a disciple	Consciousness of an undeveloped man	Consciousness of the animal kingdom	Consciousness of the vegetable kingdom
Divine Lives / *First*	*					
Divine Builders/ *Second*	*					
Lesser Builders / *Third*	*	*				
Human Hierachy/ *Fourth*	*	*	*			
Human Personality/ *Fifth*	**	**	**	*	*	
The Lunar Lords/ *sixth*	*	*	*	*	*	*
Elemental Lives/ *seventh*	*	*	*	*	*	*

* denotes includes

If we look at the seven creative hierarchies using the idea of the major three, the synthesising fourth and the three subsidiaries, the picture is as follows:

Angelic Hierarchies

1. Divine lives
2. Divine builders
3. Lesser builders
4. Human hierarchy—solar angels—synthesising and interceding

Human Hierarchies

5. Human personality: Reflecting the divine lives
6. Lunar lords: Reflecting the divine builders
7. Elemental lives: Reflecting the lesser builders

If you have a problem coming to grips with the idea of the creative hierarchies, the building bricks of our solar system, consider that when in incarnation, we ourselves comprise hierarchies VII,

VI, and V, and through our spiritual natures, are striving to become responsive to hierarchy IV. This is what distinguishes us from the animal kingdom.

The Planets

Entity manifesting: A planetary Logos
Body of manifestation: A planet **Receptive centre**: A planetary pole
Surface radiation or emanation: Planetary prana
Movement produced: Planetary rotation
Distributive effect: planetary etheric radiation (felt within the system)
The Secret Doctrine

According to esoteric tradition, a total of seventy planets preside over what *The Secret Doctrine* calls "the destiny of nations." Of these seventy, twelve are of particular importance to our planetary system.

The twelve subdivide into seven sacred and five non-sacred planets. We have met the seven and the five before. When the twelve is divided esoterically, the five serve the seven.

The sun and the moon are not counted in this tally of twelve planets. Technically, the sun is a star and not a planet, and the moon has special status, being the satellite of the Earth and a "dead" planet (see Endnote 1). Both luminaries, however, are made to stand in as substitutes for hidden planets.

Hidden planets are planets that exist in etheric matter only, and humanity is not yet able to respond fully to their energies. The majority of the seventy planets that influence our system are hidden planets. Of the hidden planets, the most important is Vulcan, which is both named and located. It orbits between the sun and Mercury.

The planets transmit all the celestial influences to which we are capable of responding. This remains the case up until a human being has in his sphere of awareness the buddhic plane (ie, after the third initiation). Then, with a foot in World Five, he is able to receive the influences coming from World Three, the zodiacal constellations, and the suns of the Milky Way.

Each planet is a threefold being, having a spiritual nature, a personality, and a body. We are told that the planets experience the same kind of conflict between their higher and lower principles as we ourselves do and that the physical body of the planet is a very low-grade entity on the involutionary arc.

As a group, the planets represent chakras in the body of "our" Solar Logos. The nonsacred planets form the lower chakras and the sacred planets the higher.

The so-called seven Heavenly Men (ie, the Logoi of the sacred planets on the second plane of our solar system) represent the spiritual attainments of the planets as a group. In this grouping, the sacred seven are served by the five nonsacred planets.

The sacred seven subdivides into the three and the four: three synthesising schemes and four schemes concerned with the development of a specific principle. In this grouping, Mercury acts as the synthesising fourth principle.

All the planets are under the dominion of the sun, the one resolver.

The Sacred and Nonsacred Planets

Planet	Status	Comments
Neptune	Sacred	*Synthesizing*
Uranus	Sacred	*Synthesizing*
Saturn	Sacred	*Synthesizing / sacred scheme for third principle*
Jupiter	Sacred	*Sacred scheme for second principle*
Venus	Sacred	*Sacred scheme for fifth principle* considered to be the Earth's twin
Mercury	Sacred	*Sacred scheme for fourth principle*
Vulcan	Sacred	*Sacred scheme for first principle* inter-Mercurial planet existing in etheric matter
The Earth	Non-sacred	*Non-sacred scheme for fourth principle* not used in conventional astrology
Mars	Non-sacred	*Non-sacred scheme for sixth principle*
Pluto	Non-sacred	*Non-sacred scheme for first principle*

In esoteric tradition, the sun and moon, used as substitutes, stand in for

- Two hidden planets, described in the *Secret Doctrine* as "planets of which humanity knows nothing." If the above chart is studied, it becomes evident that the nonsacred planets, as a group, are short of four schemes: the second, third, fifth, and seventh. We must assume that the hidden planets, in some arrangement, accommodate these schemes.
- Neptune, Uranus, and Vulcan: When the sun is the substitute, it represents the consciousness-developing aspects of these planets; when the Moon is the substitute, then it represents the form-building aspect (see Endnotes 2 and 3).

Planetary rulerships

Beings / kingdom	Ruling planet
Divine Flames	Sun
Divine Builders	Jupiter
Lesser Builders	Saturn
Human Hierarchy	Mercury
Human Personality	Venus
Lunar Lords	Mars
Elemental Lives	Moon
Kingdom of Souls	Uranus & Neptune
Human Kingdom	Mercury & Saturn
Animal Kingdom	Moon & Mars
Vegetable Kingdom	Venus & Jupiter
Mineral Kingdom	Vulcan & Pluto

The Planets as Distributors of the Rays

Ray	Distributing Planet
Ray 1	Vulcan; Pluto
Ray II	The Sun; Jupiter
Ray III	Saturn; the Earth
Ray IV	Mercury; the Moon
Ray V	Venus
Ray VI	Mars; Neptune
Ray VII	Uranus; Jupiter

Our Planet, Earth

"Our Earth, being a nonsacred planet, is in the process of becoming a sacred planet. This means an interim of upheaval, chaos and difficulty."

Esoteric Astrology

Our planet is a nonsacred planet.
Within the solar system, our planet embodies the fourth (synthesising) principle.
Our planetary Logos has a third ray soul and a fourth ray personality.
The body of the planetary Logos has three energy centres of absolute
significance for the development of consciousness: **1)** Shamballa;
2) the Hierarchy, and 3) humanity (see Endnote 4).

Spiritual Nature
The Planetary Logos

Active on the third plane (down) of our solar system; with the other nonsacred planets, it serves
the seven sacred planets and their expression, the seven Heavenly Men, on the second plane

Planetary Personality
Sanat Kumara
"The KING, The Lord of the World . . . . He it is Who . . . . authorises
what shall be done to further the ends of evolution"
—*A Treatise on Cosmic Fire*
Overshadowed by the Planetary Logos and functioning on
the fourth plane (down) of our solar system

Planetary head centre
Correspondence: Shamballa
"The most obvious force in the world today, is that of the first Ray of Will and Power . . . .
This is the force which pours into the world from the world centre, Shamballa."
—*The Destiny of Nations*
Presided over by Sanat Kumara; receives energies via the rays from the
major constellations, most significantly, the Great Bear, and distributes
to the creative hierarchies by means of the zodiacal signs

Planetary Egoic centre
Correspondence: The Hierarchy (of Masters)
"The Hierarchy is composed of Those Who have triumphed over
matter, and who have achieved the goal by the very same steps that
individuals tread today . . . (the) Elder brothers of humanity"
—*Initiation, Human and Solar*
Receives energy via the rays from the major constellations, most significantly
Sirius, and distributes by means of the planets to develop self-consciousness
in all beings; develop consciousness in the three lower kingdoms

Planetary heart centre
Correspondence: the Egos on the Mental plane

Planetary ajna centre
Correspondence: humanity

It is important be clear about the identity and the role of the Hierarchy (of Masters). Called simply the Hierarchy, it is composed of almost exclusively (now) of beings who have emerged from the ranks of the fourth kingdom in nature, hence the description the Elder Brothers of humanity. The role of the Hierarchy is to supervise the development of consciousness on our planet.

Endnotes

1. The Moon

D.K. is never more negating than when on the subject of the moon. There is a very good reason for this, in as much as the moon has no place to play in the evolution of human consciousness. D.K. describes the moon as the site of a failed system. With its first and second principles removed (by the Solar Logos), the moon is on the involutionary arc and has its own agenda. Although its effect upon the organic life of our planet is beyond dispute, the moon can distribute nothing to the Earth that can assist the development of consciousness. Indeed, to meet its own entirely involutionary purposes, it takes rather than gives and hinders rather than helps the development of human consciousness.

Students are advised to take the moon's 'deadness' on board in their interpretations and take it as a symbol of the past of what has been (see Chapter 5).

2. Chiron

Although it is not mentioned in *Esoteric Astrology,* D.K. has subsequently acknowledged that the planetoid Chiron does have a significance for the evolution of human consciousness (see Chapter 5).

3. The Hidden Planets

The hidden planets and the use of the sun and moon as substitutes does tend to add to the confusion when reading *Esoteric Astrology* because it is by no means always clear for which planet they are standing in. The implications of this for the practising astrologer are discussed in Chapter 5.

4. The Hierarchy

On this matter, C.W. Leadbeater is unsurpassed. See *The Masters and the Path.*

Chapter 3

The Worlds of Man

"We are apt to think that initiation and liberation are the achievement of the human kingdom and the attainment of humanity. This is not the case."—D.K., *Esoteric Astrology*

"Man is specially made for evolution—he is a special experiment made for self development. Every man is an experiment, not all men."—P.D. Ouspensky

Terms of relevance to this chapter

Term	Definition	Comments
Initiation	A process of developing inclusiveness. This involves the opening and coordinating of the centres or chakras	The process involves five major Initiations*(see Endnote 1)*
Undeveloped/ ordinary man	Three major chakras only open	
Developed man	In the process of opening the chakras above the diaphragm	
Aspirant	One beginning to respond to the idea of spiritual development	Up to the First Initiation
Disciple	One consciously and consistently working with the idea of spiritual development An 'accepted disciple' is one who has been accepted into a Master's Ashram or cadre	Includes Second and up to Third Initiation
Initiate	One who has taken the Third Initiation	In Esoteric tradition the Third Initiation is considered to be the first of the Initiations

Causal body	Also known as the egoic body	The vehicle of communication between the soul and the personality
Ego	Soul; centre of consciousness; conferring identity	The egoic body of a human being is formed on the upper planes of the mental plane
lotuses	the appearance of the etheric centres. The petals of the lotuses face downwards until the centre is fully opened when they reverse themselves	The number of fiery petals in each lotus is determined by the centre. The heart chakra has twelve as does its higher expression the Egoic lotus
The heart centre in the head	The crown (head) chakra has 1000 petals. Its heart is a twelve petalled lotus which represents the highest aspect of the heart centre hence the 'heart in the head'	Not to be confused with the heart centre which is midway up the spine and which is externalized in the thymus gland
Dhyan Chohan	One of seven Intelligences or Beings who can be said to be architects of the plan for our planet and under each of which is born one of the seven egoic groupings	This term is used in *The Secret Doctrine* in a way that equates the Dhyan Chohans with the seven Heavenly Men

The three, the seven, and the twelve that structure the universe are significant groupings in the structure of man: He is a threefold being having a spiritual nature, a personality and a body; he has seven major chakras; his five spinal chakras serve the seven head chakras which are open in perfected man. There are twelve types of personality expressing seven egoic groupings on the mental plane.

The Initiations

Initiation	Planetary rulers	Definition	Comments
First	Pluto and Vulcan	Control of the physical vehicle and its appetites in accordance with the dictates of conscience which is astral in nature	Removing all that hinders development in the physical and astral bodies
Second	Neptune and Mars	Control on the astral plane	Demonstrating awareness and resistance to glamour
Third	Mars and the Moon	Control on the mental plane and control of the astral body from the mental plane	Demonstrating awareness and resistance to delusion
Fourth	Mercury and Saturn	Destruction of the causal body	Re-absorption into Spirit

Fifth	Uranus and Jupiter	Reorganization of the totality of energies which make up the Initiate	Conferring immortality

The Fourth Kingdom in Nature

To recapitulate on what has been said so far about man:

- He belongs to Worlds Six and Seven, and the fourth, fifth, sixth, and seventh creative hierarchies comprise his very being and describe his field of expression when he is in incarnation. Of these four hierarchies, three can be said to condition him: the fourth, fifth, and sixth.
- Under law, each subplane of any world is en rapport with its counterpart in any other world, a human being is connected to the fourth, fifth, six, and seventh subplanes of all the worlds that comprise the universe by means of a stream of force or line of distribution. That means, for example, that the egoic centre of a man is connected to the egoic centre of the Solar Logos.
- The human personality is connected to the five creative hierarchies that are now out of manifestation, having achieved liberation in the first solar system, which are expressing themselves through the fifth creative hierarchy. As mentioned in Chapter 2, although out of manifestation the fifth creative hierarchy is communicating with the Xth (third). Thus, the human personality is the link between the present and the previous solar system. (Refer to the previous chapter and, specifically, to the table of the Seven Manifesting Hierarchies if you find the numbering confusing.)
- Through the energy centres in the human etheric vehicle, an individual is connected to all things in the universe.

Of the kingdoms in nature, the human kingdom, at present, is the only one able to reach the level of the angels. The transformative capacity of the human kingdom far greater than that of the other kingdoms and is therefore uniquely useful to both the process of evolution and that of involution. God and nature can be said to fight for the energetic output of the fourth kingdom in nature.

- Collectively, humanity corresponds to the solar plexus centre, while its most evolved members correspond the planetary ajna centre.
- Within the collectivity, which is the human family, five groupings are to be found and these express themselves through the five terrestrial zones containing five energy centres within those continents (see Endnote 2).
- The evolution of human and planetary consciousness is to be carried out through seven root races. The Aryan race is the fifth of these root races, and the sixth root race is now in the process of coming into being (see Endnote 3).

The Fifth Kingdom in Nature

The fifth kingdom in nature is the kingdom of souls or the kingdom of God. The fifth kingdom emerges from the fourth and comprises those who have the heart centre fully open. D.K. describes it as "an organised body which is already evoking recognition from those people who do seek first the kingdom of God, and discover thereby the kingdom they seek is already here."

The Reappearance of the Christ

The opening of the heart centre and the development and increase of the fifth kingdom will be the focus of the sixth root race, as the personality has been the focus of the fifth root race.

The Levels of Human Consciousness

Hierarchy/ *plane of solar system*	Inclusive awareness of perfected man	Inclusive awareness of an Initiate	Inclusive awareness of an ordinary man	Vehicles developed
Lesser Builders/ *third*	*			Atmic body
Human Hierarchy/ *fourth*	*	*		Buddhic body
Human personality/ *fifth*	*	*		ii) Egoic body
	*	*	*	i) Mental body
Lunar Lords/ *sixth*	*	*	*	Astral body
Elemental Lives/ *seventh*	*	*	*	Physical body

* Denotes sphere of consciousness includes this plane.

The Constitution of Man

The Monad, or pure spirit, the Father in Heaven
First aspect: Will or power—The Father
Second aspect: Love wisdom—The Son
Third aspect: Active intelligence—The Holy Spirit

The Monad reflects itself in:
The ego, higher self, or individuality
First aspect: Spiritual will—Atma
Second aspect: Intuition—Buddhi, Love—Wisdom, the Christ principle
Third aspect: Higher or abstract mind—Higher manas

The ego reflects itself in:

The personality or lower self, physical plane man
First aspect: The mental body Second aspect: The emotional
body Third aspect: The physical body

The Chakras

As noted above, it is the chakra system that connects a man to all that is. A human being comprises twenty-one chakras and seven major chakras.

A human being, by virtue of being a member of this kingdom, has three of the major chakras open: the centre at the base of spine, the sacral centre, and the solar plexus centre. The important spleen centre is in no way controlled by the spinal column, and for that reason, it is not considered a major chakra.

Head centre: First principle
Ajna centre: Second principle
Throat centre: Third principle

Heart centre: Fourth principle

Sacral centre: Fifth principle
Solar plexus centre: Sixth principle
Centre at the base of the spine: Seventh principle

Energy centre/chakra	Ray	Planetary distributor: *ordinary man*	Planetary distributor: *developed man*
Head	Ray I	Pluto	Vulcan
Ajna	Ray II	Venus	Venus
Throat	Ray III	Earth	Saturn
Heart	Ray II	Sun	Sun
Solar plexus	Ray VI	Mars	Neptune
Sacral	Ray VII	Uranus	Uranus
Base of Spine	Ray 1	Pluto	Pluto

The Development of Human Consciousness

The development of consciousness in a human being, as in all other beings, involves the opening of the higher chakras.

The Human Being
Entity manifesting: The thinker, a Dhyan Chohan
Body of manifestation: Physical body
Receptive centre: The spleen surface
Radiation or emanation: Health aura

Movement produced: Atomic rotation
Distributive effect: Human etheric radiation (felt by environment)
The Secret Doctrine

In an undeveloped human being, the flow of energy is from the head centre
to the base of the spine. Only the lower three centres are open.

In one actively involved in spiritual development, the lower centres are returning energy to the
higher, and the lower centres become fused with the higher. The solar plexus fuses with and opens
the heart centre; the sacral centre fuses with and opens the throat centre.
The ajna centre then integrates the hitherto uncoordinated personality.
This is known as transmutation.

In a human being in whom the head centre has been opened, the flow is once again downward
through the fused centres and the centre at the base of the spine becomes fully activated.
This is known as transformation.

It will be noted that the passage of force through the human vehicle conforms to the universal
pattern: distribution, return, transformation, and redistribution.

Centre	Status	Comments
Head	Organ of spiritual triad	Gives consciousness of buddhic plane
Ajna	Integrates: i) personality conciousness ii) the personality and the soul. When these two stages are complete, the reflection of the spiritual triad in the personality is complete	Integrates buddhic and mental planes
Throat	Organ of spiritual triad	Gives consciousness of mental plane
Heart	Organ of spiritual triad	Integrates mental and astral planes. The first of the higher centres i.e. centres above the diaphragm
Solar plexus	Organ of personality	Gives consciousness of astral plane
Sacral centre	Organ of personality	Gives consciousness of physical plane
Centre at base of spine	Organ of personality	Integrates buddhic and physical planes which then gives consciousness of the atmic plane i.e. Nirvana

D.K. gives the details of the process of integration as follows:

Transmutation

From the sacral centre to the throat centre:
Physical creation is transmuted into artistic creativity.
From the solar centre to the heart centre: Individual emotional
consciousness is transmuted into group consciousness.
From the base of the spine to the head centre: Material force is transmuted into spiritual energy.
From any or all of the five spinal centres to the ajna centre: Uncoordinated
living is transmuted into personality integration.
From the six centres in relationship to the higher head centre:
Personality activity is transmuted into spiritual living.

This is a wide generalisation, and the process is not carried forward in any sequential fashion or smoothly and as the above tabulation might suggest. The process involved is spread over many lifetimes of unconscious transmutation in the earlier stages. As a result of bitter experience and of conscious effort in the later stages, it becomes increasingly dynamic and effective as the various stages upon the path are trodden by the aspirant.

Transformation Leading to Transfiguration

Once the head centre is awakening and the disciple is consciously active in the work of directing the energies to the centres and thereby governing the personality life, there is a scientific undertaking of energising the centres in a certain-ordered rhythm.

1. The stage of energising the creative life via the throat centre, thus bringing:
   a. the head centre and throat centre
   b. these two and the sacral centre
   c. all three, consciously and simultaneously, into conscious relation

2. The stage of energising the conscious life of relationships via the heart centre, thus bringing:
   a. the head centre and heart centre
   b. these two and the solar plexus centre
   c. all three, simultaneously and consciously, into close cooperation

3. The stage of energising the entire man, via the basic centre thus bringing:
   a. the head centre and basic centre
   b. these two and the ajna centre
   c. all three, simultaneously and consciously, into rhythmic, coordinated expression. This is a final stage of great importance and only takes place in its completeness at the time of the third initiation, that of the transfiguration.

Esoteric Healing

In both processes (transmutation and transformation), the five rays with which a disciple has to work have a definite active effect, and karmic adjustments provide either opportunities or hindrances.

The five rays of the disciple are:

- ◆ Soul ray: Conditioning
- ◆ Personality ray: Conditioning
- ◆ Ray of the mental body: Subsidiary
- ◆ Ray of the astral body: Subsidiary
- ◆ Ray of the physical body: Subsidiary

After the third initiation, the subsidiary rays lose their importance. There are then three conditioning rays:

- ◆ Monadic ray
- ◆ Soul ray
- ◆ Personality ray

Ouspensky summarises the stages involved in opening the chakras accordingly:

Automaton working by external influences *start point*	Desires produced by automaton *stage one*	Thoughts proceeding from desires *stage two*	Different and contradictory wills created by desires *stage three*

Body obeying desires and emotions which are subject to intelligence *stage seven*	Emotional powers and desires obeying thought and intelligence *stage six*	Thinking function obeying consciousness and will *stage five*	I Ego Consciousness Will *stage four*

The Egoic Body

Another name for this vehicle is the causal body, so-called because it holds the cause of all things in itself. It is not subject to external influences, which we call fate.

The egoic body embodies the fourth principle. It synthesises the achievements of the three lower bodies: the physical, astral, and mental. It itself acts as the mediator between the highest and lowest aspects of man. Its creation on the mental plane precedes the first initiation. It garners and confers coherence upon the experiences of lifetimes and enables the individual human soul to emerge from the group soul of the human family.

The causal body forms the bridge between the soul and the personality. It enables the process of individuation to turn into that of liberation.

It is formed upon the three highest subplanes of the mental plane (which is, of course, a subplane of the cosmic physical plane).

D.K. gives the properties of the causal body as follows:

- ◆ The vehicle of manifestation of a solar angel who is its informing life and who is in the process of constructing it, of perfecting it and enlarging it, and thus reflecting on a tiny scale the work of the Logos on His own plane.

- ♦ A collection of permanent atoms, three in all, enclosed in an envelope of mental essence
- ♦ The product of millennia of lives of pain and endeavour
- ♦ A body which turns from a colourless ovoid, holding the ego like a yolk within an eggshell, to a thing of rare beauty, containing within itself all the colours of the rainbow. It will develop an inner irradiation and an inner flame that will then work from the centre to the periphery and burn up the body, enabling it to become reabsorbed in spiritual consciousness.

The Goals of Man

Individuation

The goal of the fourth kingdom in nature is individuation. This is achieved during the second initiation or Ouspensky's stage four (see above).

This is the experience encapsulated in the sign Leo. The heart centre has opened as the result of the transformation of solar plexus energy, and this enables fusion between the lower and higher aspects of the personality and gives colour and content to the causal body.

The process of transmuting solar plexus energy and opening the heart centre is assisted by the ideas and teachings released by the hierarchy. This has characterised spiritual activity among the fifth root race. The keynote has been devotionalism.

We are told that in those making up the sixth root race that the heart chakra is already open and the petals of the heart lotus are upward and not downward pointing. This means that the spirituality of the sixth root race will be concerned with creating the fusion between the heart and the head centres. The emphasis will be upon the development of spiritual will (see Endnote 4).

The Alignment of the Soul and the Personality

The more advanced stages of a man's development (which can be said to commence when the soul and personality are aligned) are the attainment, not of humanity, but of the soul which has at last succeeded in dominating the personality and in manifesting its true nature and character in spite of the personality and what D.K. calls "the antagonism of the human being intent upon his own purposes."

The soul communicates with the personality it now controls via the causal body. This is achieved at the third initiation. As the throat and sacral centre have now fused, a period of soul controlled creative activity then ensues. This is the stage at which the initiate can be used as an instrument of the Hierarchy.

This stage ends with the fourth initiation when the causal body is burned up, and the initiate is now the agent of Shamballa and of spiritual will.

Endnotes

1. The Initiations

In recent years, the initiations have proved to be a matter that has given rise to much misunderstanding. The principal problem is that trends in New Age thinking have encouraged aspirants to assume that they have attained a far higher level than is the case. The very fact that such misunderstanding can arise is evidence that neither those putting out the ideas nor those receiving them have yet reached the third initiation and mastered glamour and delusion.

D.K. has indeed encouraged disciples to take their eyes off transfiguration and anticipate the higher initiations because, as he says, "Whatsoever man has desired, ever he has had," but he did *not* say assume oneself to be of that level.

2. Planetary centres

Terrestrial Zone	Centre	Dominant Ray
The Continent of Europe	Geneva	Ray II
The British Commonwealth	London	Ray I
The Continent of America	New York	Ray VI
Central and Western Asia	Darjeeling	Ray I
The Far East	Tokyo	Ray I

Region	Soul Ray	Personality Ray
The Occident	Ray II	Ray IV
The Orient	Ray IV	Ray III

3. The root races

Root race	Ray	Planetary grouping	Correspondence with Centre	Goal
First	I	Shamballa	Head	Will
Second	VII	Deva	Sacral	Responsiveness
Third	III	Animal Kingdom	Throat	Intellect
Fourth	VI	Vegetable Kingdom	Solar Plexus	Instinct
Fifth	V	Humanity	Ajna	Intuition
Sixth	II	Kingdom of Souls	Heart	Love
Seventh	I & VII	Shamballa & the Mineral Kingdom	Head & base of spine	Synthesis

4.   The chakras and the glands

Energy centre/chakra	Externalised in gland
Head Centre	Pineal
Ajna	Pituitary
Throat	Thyroid
Heart	Thymus
Solar plexus	Pancreas
Sacral	The gonads
Base of spine	Adrenal

Anyone wanting to read further into the matter of the energy centres and the physical vehicle should read Alice Bailey's *Esoteric Healing*.

Part Two

Adapting Orthodox Language

"The key to the whole process as far as the Earth is concerned—and the individual on the Earth—is to be found in the words: *transcending*—the transcending cause; *transmitting*—the zodiacal signs; *transforming*—the sun and the soul; *transfiguring*—the planets." *Esoteric Astrology*

The aim of this section is to begin the task of integrating the techniques and understanding of conventional or orthodox astrology with esoteric perspectives.

There is no value in waving the flag for pure esoteric astrology when, as a discipline, it does not address the perceived problems and questions of the people who turn to astrology for guidance. This has been a very evident problem in recent years. Alice Bailey's *Esoteric Astrology* has been studied and reproduced and the information contained within it presented every which way, but the fact is that it has not been made to work to any great effect at the level of everyday living because it is too far in advance of where we are at present. For as long as we see our problems as occurring in the outer world rather than arising in our own consciousness, we need a branch of astrology that can deal with form.

Orthodox astrology is able to supply us with most of what we require, provided we can supply it with the kind of concepts that will make it yield the information that we seek in a horoscope.

It has long been fashionable in spiritual circles to denigrate orthodox astrology. The problem, though, is not the discipline per se, but low levels of understanding and technical knowledge amongst practitioners.

It is not always understood that astrology is only a tool; it can supply answers only to the questions we put through it. It is up to the practitioners to frame useful questions, and learn how to find the answers (see Endnote 1). This requirement is demonstrated most obviously in horary astrology where the quality of the question formulated will determine usefulness and often the very intelligibility of the answer.

After the tour through God's anatomy that constituted Part One, it should be something of a relief to be back on more familiar territory, if that term is permissible. But Part One will have done its work if it has decentralised perspectives, to some degree, and implanted the awareness that as members of the human family, we are not, to use D.K.'s expression, "factors of isolated importance."

It is customary to put the Sun and the Moon into the upper case when referring to the astrologer's tools, as distinct from the physical entities. This we are doing in this work from hereon, where our concern is horoscopical interpretation.

Endnotes

1. We will be raising this matter again in Part Three, where we will be considering the concepts an esoterically oriented astrologer can use to good effect.

Chapter 4

Looking Again at the Zodiacal Signs

"In the understanding of the significance of the distinction between constellations as galaxies of stars and signs as concentrated influences will come fresh insights into the science of astrology."

"The twelve signs serve as focal points for certain forces and enable the individual to be in touch with great reservoirs of energy that then definitely condition him."
—*Esoteric Astrology*

Recapitulating on World Three

We established in Chapter 1 that the suns and constellations of the Milky Way belong to World Three, the world to which the absolute monad distributes.

World Three sends energy in the form of consciousness to World Two, which transforms it and then returns it to World Three. World Three then transmits to, the world of the planets.

The constellations of the Milky Way, therefore, belong to the first triad, the triad of spirit; the zodiacal signs that concentrate the influences of the twelve zodiacal constellations must be considered to be the representatives in our world of the first triad. The planets, by comparison, belong to the second triad, the triad of soul.

This distinction is of considerable importance in understanding the relation of the planets to the signs and their relative strengths as sources of influence. It is not a distinction that has been well made in conventional astrology, but it is a distinction central to our study.

Zodiacal energies pass through Shamballa. They are related to the first ray of will or power and affect the human Monad. They are representatives of a world higher than that of the planets, and their influence increases as the "instrument of receptivity" increases its vibrational rate. As D.K. repeats at intervals throughout *Esoteric Astrology,* "The type of mechanism and the quality of the consciousness determine the result."

As far as that instrument of receptivity, a human being, is concerned, it means that the more highly developed he becomes, the greater becomes the influence of the signs and of World Three. In their strengthening light, that of the planets eventually fades out. This means, of course, that the ray transmitted by a sign will replace that transmitted by any planet posited within that sign.

As this becomes the state of affairs at the third initiation, and not before, this statement is not of much practical value to the practising astrologer (see Endnote 1), but it is useful in illustrating the point that needs to be understood

about the relative strength of the signs and planets and the variables introduced by different levels of consciousness.

In horoscopy, the zodiacal signs are the repository of will whilst the planets are the agents of consciousness. The zodiacal signs are the representatives of a higher world whose influence remains very largely dormant until a man, in the course of his development, has his head centres opened.

Orthodox astrology has captured and described those influences from each of the signs to which the average person is receptive. Esoteric astrology, anticipating a higher level of receptivity, adds other features that should be used as supplements to the conventional wisdom.

Certain of these supplementary features are given in the supplement to this chapter.

The Zodiacs

It should be recalled that World Two, which returns energy to World Three, is the world of the major constellations. The energy that World Three transmits to World Five, therefore, is blended with that of a still higher world, the world from which the seven rays can be said to originate.

This blend creates a total of twelve basic energies (seven from the stars of the Great Bear, two from Sirius, and three from the Pleiades) that express themselves through the twelve constellations.

When these twelve ecliptical constellations are considered from the point of view of the development of consciousness on our planet, they become the zodiacal signs (see Chapter 1, Endnote 3; also Endnote 2, below).

When considering the distribution of force through the universe, talk about constellations. When assessing the impact of the energy of World Three upon the development of consciousness upon our planet, talk about zodiacal signs.

The Greater Zodiac
The succession of the greater rounds of the zodiac over a period of approximately
250,000 years has a correspondence to the life cycle of the human monad.
The progress of the sun as it passes through the signs of the zodiac during one of these
cycles (averaging 25,000 years) finds its analogy in the life cycle of the ego or soul.

The Lesser Zodiac
The lesser round, which is the result of an illusion and seemingly covered by the sun
in the course of a year, corresponds to the life of the personality. The lesser zodiac is a
reflection of the greater zodiac. What applies to the greater zodiac will find its reflection
in the lesser zodiac, which is the basis of horoscopy as we practise it in the West.

The Divisions of the Greater Zodiac

Seven of the zodiacal signs are related to the unfoldment of planetary consciousness on Earth and only incidentally involving the human hierarchy (IVth creative hierarchy). These signs are Aries, Taurus, Gemini, Virgo, Libra, Sagittarius, and Aquarius.

Five signs are related to the unfoldment in time and space of the human family: Cancer, Leo, Scorpio, Capricorn, and Pisces.

These five signs are related in the planetary sense to:
- the five great races (of which the Aryan is the fifth)
- the five continents (Europe, Africa, Asia, Australasia, and America)
- the five major endocrine glands (base of the spine, sacral, solar plexus, heart, and throat)

According to esoteric tradition, four signs convey the required energy to make humanity divine: Aries, Leo, Scorpio, and Aquarius.

Five signs are considered to be particularly influential in the life of the advanced disciple: Libra, Sagittarius, Taurus, Pisces, and Aquarius.

The Cosmic Triangles

"The Science of Triangles concerns the beneficence of deity, and through the intricate combination of cosmic, systemic and planetary triangles, the purposes of God are working out."
-Esoteric Astrology

In every triplicity, there are three major qualities manifesting or, put another way, three basic energies seeking expression and influence. The importance of the triad was emphasised in Part One where we were concerned with the structure of the universe. In this part of the work, we are concerned with the triad from the point of view of consciousness and development (see Endnote 3).

All triangles of energy noted in this section will be regarded as expressing:
- major conditioning energy producing manifestation and corresponding to the Monad aspect: life
- secondary qualifying energy producing consciousness and corresponding to the ego or soul aspect: quality
- lesser expression of force, producing tangibility, and corresponding to the personality aspect: appearance

Of the twelve zodiacal signs, three are considered to rule the remaining nine. These three signs are sometimes called the cosmic decanates, and they are to the greater zodiac what the planets are to the decanates of the signs:
- Scorpio, which is the sign of Hercules and confers strength through testing and struggle
- Taurus, which is the sign of the Buddha and confers illumination

> ♦ Pisces, which is the sign of the Christ and brings about resurrection through sacrifice

Another triangle of cosmic energy is known to be concerned with the unfolding of human consciousness in its three aspects. According to D.K, these signs are known esoterically as "the producers of that which knows, the informers of that which is awakened and the constructors of the modes of fusing. They shatter that which they have produced only to produce it in greater beauty and a wider fullness."

> ♦ Leo creates the self-consciousness of the individual
> ♦ Virgo creates the recognition of the Christ life in the disciple
> ♦ Pisces creates awareness of a universal nature in the initiate

In *Esoteric Astrology,* D.K. identifies various other triangles of influence that directly affect the development of human consciousness. They affect humanity as whole and, by correspondence, those individuals within the human family who are awakening.

These include:

Triangle of initiations:
> ♦ Scorpio (strength through testing)
> ♦ Taurus (illumination)
> ♦ Pisces (sacrifice)

Triangle of crisis:
> ♦ Leo (individuation)
> ♦ Libra (reversal)
> ♦ Capricorn (initiation).

Triangle of humanity:
> ♦ Taurus (illumined consciousness)
> ♦ Leo (self-consciousness)
> ♦ Aquarius (man of spirit)

Triangle of the solar angel:
> ♦ Gemini (functioning of dual mind)
> ♦ Libra (point of balance; past/future)
> ♦ Aquarius (activity of the mind which has been initiated into the universal mind).

As the lesser zodiac has a correspondence with the greater zodiac, recognising these triangles of influence in charts, when emphasised by occupying planets, should become part of horoscopical interpretation.

The Cosmic Crosses

"The Inner web of light which is called the etheric body of our planet is
essentially a web of triangles and when the evolutionary process is completed,
it will have been organised. At present a pattern of squares is the major
construction, but this is slowly changing as the divine plan works out."

"It is through the squares or the quadernial relation that the form aspect
is brought into relation and adequacy with the will of deity, expressing
itself through the gradually unfolding consciousness aspect."
-Esoteric Astrology

All evolving beings progress by means of the crosses that are three in number. As far as a man is concerned, the crosses govern all seven stages of his development, from incarnation to the burning ground.

The mutable cross is the cross of the Holy Spirit, the cross of the body or form nature.
This cross transforms animal man into the aspirant. It is the cross of
the personality upon which a man first integrates as a human being in
response to circumstance and then in response to the soul.
Experience upon the mutable cross integrates a man into the planetary centre called humanity.
The arms of this cross are Gemini, Virgo, Sagittarius, and Pisces.

The fixed cross is the cross of God, the cross of the soul.
On this cross, a man becomes fixed in purpose and sensitive to the larger
whole, first as a probationary and then as an accepted disciple.
Experience upon this cross integrates the disciple into the planetary centre called the Hierarchy.
The arms of this cross are Taurus, Leo, Scorpio, and Aquarius.

The cardinal cross is the cross of the Risen Christ, the cross of the initiation.
This cross is mounted when Nirvana is entered. Those on this cross are in the
process of unfolding a higher level of being. The scope and cycle of its influence
are unknown, even to our planetary Logos who is Himself stretched upon it.
Experience upon this cross integrates the initiate into the planetary centre called Shamballa.
The arms of this cross are Aries, Cancer, Libra, and Capricorn.

During the course of his development, a man passes through seven stages or crises.

Crisis	Consciousness	Zodiacal sign	Quality
Incarnation	Individualisation	Cancer	Cardinal
Orientation	Reversal	Aries	Cardinal
Initiation	Expansion	Capricorn	Cardinal
Renunciation	Crucifixion	Gemini	Mutable
The Battlefield	Conflict	Scorpio	Fixed
The Birthplace	Initiation	Virgo	Mutable
The Burning Ground	Liberation	Leo	Fixed

He passes through these seven crises a total of three times (ie, on each of the crosses):

- once as a self-conscious man emerging from the mass (mutable cross)
- once as an aspirant emerging out of the group of world individuals (fixed cross)
- once as an initiate as he emerges out of the ranks of world disciples (cardinal cross)

The idea of the crosses can be introduced to horoscopy to provide one of its most useful tools, but as you may suspect, the technique is rather more complicated than simply counting the number of planets in each quality. This matter will be dealt with in Chapter 4.

The Zodiac and the Rays

"The seven rays express themselves in our solar system as the
custodians or exponents of the will aspect of deity."
Esoteric Astrology

The seven rays enter our solar system via the zodiacal constellations. Each ray transmits itself through three signs. Although this information was given in Chapter 1, we reproduce it below for the purpose of convenience, and emphasise those signs which are directly related to the efforts of the creative hierarchy which is fifth down, the human personality.

- The first aspect expresses the will, which conquers and initiates.
- The second aspect expresses the will, which brings fulfilment.
- The third aspect expresses the will, which conquers death.

Ray	First Aspect	Second Aspect	Third Aspect
Ray I	Aries	**Leo**	**Capricorn**
Ray II	Gemini	Virgo	**Pisces**
Ray III	**Cancer**	Libra	**Capricorn**
Ray IV	Taurus	**Scorpio**	Sagittarius
Ray V	**Leo**	Sagittarius	Aquarius
Ray VI	Virgo	Sagittarius	**Pisces**
Ray VII	Aries	Cancer	**Capricorn**

The following details are offered as points of interest:

- **Cancer:** The creative hierarchy, which is governed by the sign Cancer, is out of manifestation, but coming into activity upon the cosmic astral plane and linked by correspondence to the human personality on the fifth plane (down).
- **Leo:** This sign governs the divine flames on the first plane (down) of our solar system, which are in etheric but not dense physical bodies. They have a special connection with the elemental lives on the seventh plane (down).
- **Scorpio:** This sign governs the human hierarchy on the fourth plane (down) of our solar system.
- **Capricorn:** This sign governs the human personality.

♦ **Pisces:** The creative hierarchy governed by this sign is also out of manifestation but is active on the cosmic astral plane and influences the beings on the second and sixth planes (down).

Presented in a more user-friendly form is the connection between the rays and the signs:

Zodiacal Sign	Rays	Traditional names	Blend of qualities
Aries	I & VII	Will to Power & Cermonial Magic	Initiation & expression
Taurus	IV	Harmony through Conflict	Harmonisation
Gemini	II	Love-Wisdom	Unification
Cancer	III & VII	Active Intelligence & Ceremonial Magic	Evolution & expression
Leo	I & V.	Will to Power & Concrete Science	Initiation & action
Virgo	II & VI	Love-Wisdom & Devotion	Unification & causation
Libra	III	Active Intelligence	Evolution
Scorpio	IV	Harmony through Conflict	Harmonisation
Sagittarius	IV, V & VI	Harmony through Conflict, Concrete Science & Devotion	Harmonisation, action & causation
Capricorn	I, III & VII	Will to Power, Active Intelligence & Ceremonial Magic	Initiation, evolution & expression
Aquarius	V	Concrete Science	Action
Pisces	II & VI	Love-Wisdom & Devotion	Unification & causation

With this information in the forefront of the mind, we will now look at each of the signs. Clearly, the qualities conferred by the rays they transmit have conditioned understanding of the signs, even though orthodox astrology knows nothing of the rays.

It may already be apparent to you why the signs should indicate potential and why in horoscopy the Sun sign in particular describes the way forward in any lifetime. The signs are the representative of a higher level, the level of spirit. They transmit the will of God, and to that extent, they confer purpose.

The Zodiacal Signs

The Passage around the Zodiac

In *Esoteric Astrology,* D.K. states that in his involutionary stage (ie, on the mutable cross), man caught up in nature and regresses, as does the first point of Aries, through the signs, commencing in Cancer (the sign in which the crisis of incarnation occurs) and concluding in Leo. Then comes the moment of reversal (which may take a number of lifetimes), after which he proceeds in the opposite direction from Aries through to Pisces. It is helpful to think of the soul beginning to wind the man back in by means of a strengthening thread of consciousness.

D.K. makes much of this in *Esoteric Astrology,* and it always must be remembered that *Esoteric Astrology* is concerned primarily with Everyman, with the World Aspirant and the World Disciple, who are, of course, significantly less well-developed than certain individuals.

For a practising astrologer with an esoteric emphasis, this idea of the reversing wheel is unlikely to be of much practical help as a conceptual tool because he is unlikely to be attracting clients who are on the mutable cross. In consequence, there would not seem to be too much point in dwelling excessively on the detail which pertains to the wheel before it has reversed. Orthodox astrology, in fatalist, predetermined mode, services that requirement that is not our concern (see Endnote 4). It is more important that we learn how to proceed as esoteric astrologers, assuming that the wheel has been reversed and that man is travelling forward in the order of the signs. This means that a man is prepared for the experience in any one sign by his cumulative experiences in the signs previous to it. The journey from Aries to Pisces involves slow unfolding in the personality of soul awareness.

The Decanates

The decanates are said to express the personality, soul, and spirit of each of the signs. They are a correspondence on a lower level of the first, second, and third aspects as they express themselves through the zodiac.

The significance of this in horoscopy is that in each decanate, a man has experiences that will benefit his personality, soul, or spirit according to whether the influence is coming from the first, second, or third decanate. This is known to orthodox astrology, but gains a greater significance in an esoteric context.

As will be seen in the following chapter, each of the planets also expresses the three aspects, so it is important to be able to distinguish the two. The use of the term "decanates" when referring to the signs assists this.

Working with the Signs

The advice is to hold on to all that conventional astrology has taught you about the qualities of the signs, and add to that knowledge the new, esoteric qualities.

In assessing the effects of a sign, esoterically understood, upon man, there is no need to depart from the interpretive conventions of orthodox astrology.

- ♦ The planets, working through the houses, determine the form and are the paramount influence.
- ♦ The signs provide the conditioning influence. They qualify and modify the effects of the planets, as adjectives and adverbs qualify nouns and verbs.

But esoteric astrology introduces another perspective. The influence of the signs increases in direct proportion to a man's capacity to hold down the planets and receive the influence flowing through them, rather than the energy of the planets themselves (see Chapter 5).

Endnotes

1. People who seek guidance from a spiritually oriented astrologer are likely to be either aspirants or disciples. For them, therefore, the dominant influence will be the planetary, not the zodiacal.

2. We like this crisp statement, made nearly eighty years ago, by Charles Carter, the first principal of the British Astrological Faculty. It is likely to be appreciated by anyone who has been confronted with the joyless task of explaining the astrological perspective to the scientist!

> "The signs of zodiac are not the same as the constellations (groups of fixed stars) that bear the same names. At one time they were coincident, but owing to what is called the Precession of the Equinoxes, this is no longer the case, so that, for example, the two wellknown stars in the constellation Gemini, Castor and Pollux, are in the sign Cancer. The supposed ignorance of astrologers concerning the phenomenon of precession is often attacked by astronomers, though it is difficult to see upon what grounds, other than complete ignorance of astrological doctrine."
> *The Principles of Astrology*, published by the Theosophical Publishing House, 1925

3. By means of the following interlocking triangles, a man is linked to God:

Great Bear
Sirius
The Pleiades

Leo
Pisces
Capricorn

Saturn
Uranus
Mercury

Planetary head centre: Shamballa
Planetary heart centre: the Hierarchy
Planetary ajna centre: Humanity

Disciple's head centre
Disciple's heart centre
Disciple's ajna centre

Base of spine
Solar plexus
Throat centre

4. Although it has long been the fashion in the West to decry fatalistic and predictive astrology, there are probably no astrologers in the world more technically proficient than the Hindu astrologers taught to analyse a man's fate, and their skills and disciplines deserve our respect.

Chapter 5

Looking Again at the Planets

"Ordinary humanity is ruled by exoteric planets; advanced
humanity, disciples; and initiates by the esoteric planets."

"The horoscope, built round the Sun sign, is adequate for ordinary humanity. The exoteric
planets rule and man lives within the limitations of the twelve houses. The horoscope built
round the rising sign, with the esoteric planets ruling, will convey the
destiny of the disciple. As I told you, the disciple will later be responding
to the influences of the twelve arms of the three crosses as they pour their
influence through the esoteric planetary rulers via the twelve houses."
-Esoteric Astrology

To date, awareness of the discipline of esoteric astrology has been confined very largely to the existence of the rays and the matter of esoteric planetary rulerships. Information on the esoteric rulerships is now quite readily available, although far less readily
available is insight into how, precisely, in horoscopy, the esoteric rulers are to be used.

In this chapter, which is given over to the planets, we will be looking at the role of the planets in the kind of esoterically oriented horoscopical interpretation that has relevance and value at the present time. There is little value in waving the flag for pure esoteric astrology when, as a discipline, it does not address the perceived problems and questions of the people who turn to astrology for guidance.

Firstly, let us remind ourselves of the nature and the context of our relationship with the planets.

- ♦ The planets belong to World Five. They receive forces transmitted by World Three, the world of the Milky Way.
- ♦ They then send this energy to the sun (World Four), which returns it to the planets. The planets distribute to the World Seven, which includes ourselves as separate units.
- ♦ Our output then becomes part of the collective output of World Six, life on Earth. The planets, therefore, are both transmitters and transformers.
- ♦ There are seven sacred planets and five nonsacred planets. The five serve the seven, and the spiritual identity of the planets as a group are found on the second plane of our solar system in the form of the seven

Heavenly Men or the "Seven Spirits before the Throne of God" (see Endnote 1). The twelve planetary Logoi function on the buddhic plane (the fourth plane and domain of the solar angels), which is accessible to a man with his head centres opened. The planets, therefore, may be said to be the bridge between man and the Heavenly Men. For a man, the planets are the means of spiritual transformation.

♦ The seven sacred planets are each the agent of one of the seven rays. Five of these seven rays are subcontracted to the five nonsacred planets. The missing rays are fifth and seventh. These rays are not fielded by the nonsacred planets known to astrology, although you are invited to consider whether Chiron may not be fulfilling this role at this time.

Conventional astrology focuses upon the role of planets as transmitters. By means of the conventional rulerships, mankind is linked to the zodiacal signs. The rulerships assigned by conventional astrology deal with the connection between the personalities or first aspect of the signs, planets, and man. Orthodox astrology, therefore, is concerned with the way that the higher influences the lower (ie, with the downward flow of force).

The esoteric rulerships express the second or consciousness aspect and focus upon the connection between the soul of the sign, the soul of the planet, and the soul of man. Esoteric astrology, therefore, is concerned with the planets and with man in the capacity of transformers (ie, with the process of returning energies). The hierarchical rulers express the third aspect, or the product of the synthesis between life and quality. This knowledge adds an inner dimension to the horoscope

From this perspective, let us look again at the planets. As with the zodiacal signs, the advice is to add to, rather than replace the conventional wisdom about the planets. These new associations do not change the essential nature of the planet: What conventional astrology tells us about the planets as energy principles serves the esoteric approach also. What the esoteric associations do is increase the versatility of each of the planets, alerting us to the fact that orthodox astrology has encouraged the development of what, with justification, astrologer Warren Kenton calls "astrological clichés," which we have to go beyond if we are to get to grips with the insights of esoteric astrology.

The Planets and the Rays

This information has been given elsewhere, but we will bring it together in tabular form for the purposes of clarity and convenience.

Planet	Status	Ray
Vulcan	Sacred	I
Mercury	Sacred	IV
Venus	Sacred	V
Jupiter	Sacred	II
Saturn	Sacred	III
Uranus	Sacred	VII
Neptune	Sacred	VI
The Earth	Non-sacred	III
Mars	Non-sacred	VI
Pluto	Non-sacred	I
Sun	Non-sacred	II
Moon	Non-sacred	IV

The planets as rulers of the decanates

Sign	1st decanate	2nd decanate	3rd decanate
Aries	Jupiter	Sun	Mars
Taurus	Moon or Venus	Mercury	Saturn
Gemini	Jupiter	Mars	Sun
Cancer	Venus	Mercury	Moon
Leo	Sun	Jupiter	Mars
Virgo	Mercury	Saturn	Taurus
Libra	Jupiter	Saturn	Mercury
Scorpio	Mars	Sun	Venus
Sagittarius	Jupiter	Mars	Sun
Capricorn	Saturn	Taurus	Sun
Aquarius	Saturn	Mercury	Venus
Pisces	Jupiter	Moon	Mars

Planetary rulerships

Planet	Orthodox ruler of:	Esoteric Ruler of:	Hierarchical Ruler of:
Vulcan	n/a	Taurus	Taurus
Mercury	Gemini & Virgo	Aries	Scorpio
The Earth	n/a	Sagittarius	Gemini
Venus	Taurus & Libra	Gemini	Capricorn
Mars	Aries & Scorpio	Scorpio	Sagittarius
Jupiter	Sagittarius & Pisces	Aquarius	Virgo
Saturn	Capricorn & Aquarius	Capricorn	Libra
Uranus	Aquarius	Libra	Aries
Neptune	Pisces	Cancer	Cancer
Pluto	Scorpio	Pisces	Pisces
Sun	Leo	Leo	Leo
Moon	Cancer	Virgo	Aquarius

The planets and the three aspects of the zodiacal signs

Planet	Expresses first aspect of	Expresses second aspect of	Expresses third aspect of
Mercury	i)Gemini ii)Virgo	Aries	Scorpio
Venus	i)Taurus ii)Libra	Gemini	Capricorn
Mars	i)Aries ii)Scorpio	Scorpio	Sagittarius
Jupiter	Sagittarius	Aquarius	Virgo
Saturn	i)Capricorn ii)Aquarius	Capricorn	Libra
Uranus	Aquarius	Libra	Aries
Neptune	Pisces	Cancer	Cancer
Pluto	Scorpio	Pisces	Pisces

To this list should be added:
♦ Vulcan expresses the second and third aspects of the sign Taurus.
♦ The Earth expresses the second aspect of Sagittarius.

And of course:

♦ The Sun (and veiled planets: see below) express all three aspects of the sign Leo.
♦ The moon (and veiled planets) express the first, second, and third aspect of Cancer.

The esoteric astrologer needs to appreciate the interconnectedness of all things. An individual man or woman born with, for example, the sign Scorpio or any of the planetary agents of Scorpio prominent in his or her chart, will be connected in a very real way to the human Hierarchy on the fourth plane (down) of our solar system, which the sign Scorpio rules. The same applies if Mercury in a chart is found in the sign Scorpio, because Mercury is the ruler of the human Hierarchy, hence the importance of the sign Scorpio at a particular stage of development. In the same way, those with the signs Aries, Taurus, Gemini, or Pisces (and the planetary agents of those signs) prominent are connected, albeit remotely, to those creative hierarchies on the cosmic astral plane whose influence reaches us via the human personality. These connections will not be made all at once. They are the product of contemplation. Keep the charts on hand and refer to them often, and draw up your own to aid comprehension.

The Veils

The idea of the aspects of the signs enables the somewhat obscure matter of the veiled planets to which reference is made in *Esoteric Astrology* and other theosophical publications to be made rather more clear.

The veiled planets are Uranus, Neptune, and Vulcan. They are to be distinguished from the hidden planets that exist in etheric matter, whose numbers are said to be around seventy and of which four are held to be of particular importance to humanity, even though, with the exception of Vulcan, their identity is not known to us (see Chapter 1).

The veiled planets are all sacred planets to which undeveloped humanity is unreceptive, responding instead to the lower corresponding vibration of their nonsacred blinds.

- o   The Sun is a veil or a blind for the planets that express the second (soul / transforming) and third (spirit / transcending) aspects of the sign Leo.
- o   The Moon is a veil or blind for the planets that express the first (personality / transmitting), second (soul / transforming), and third (spirit / transcending) aspects of Cancer.

Technically, the Moon is *always* a blind in pure esoteric astrology. As it is a dead planet, it has no vital principles and can be said to rule only the dense physical vehicle, as distinct from the etheric vehicle, which according to esoteric understanding, is not a principle.

Sign	First aspect expressed by:	Second aspect expressed by:	Third aspect expressed by:
Leo	Sun corresponding to the physical Sun. *Ruling: Fire by friction*	Neptune (veiled by Sun) corresponding to the heart of the Sun *Ruling: Solar fire*	Uranus (veiled by Sun) corresponding to the central spiritual Sun *Ruling: Electric fire*
Cancer	Vulcan (veiled by Moon) *Ruling the physical vehicle i.e. the etheric body and specifically the solar plexus*	Neptune (veiled by Moon) *Ruling the astral vehicle i.e. the astral body and specifically the heart centre*	Uranus (veiled by Moon) *Ruling the mental vehicle i.e. the mental body and specifically the egoic or causal body*

The veils are a practical matter to the esoteric astrologer engaged in horoscopical interpretation, and they raise the issue of how to identify the planet that is being veiled. One solution that is the recognition of themes which indicate the level of development of the subject. We will look at this matter, *inter alia,* in the section that follows.

In connection with the veiled planets, there is another matter of which the astrologer has to be aware, and that is that the hidden planets represent what D.K. calls a "fluid area" in a chart. In this area, during the course of a lifetime, a person may upgrade his vehicle and therefore the energy he is able to receive. There may be a shift from the solar plexus to the heart centre, and from fire by friction to solar fire.

Working with the Planets in Horoscopy

The planets as energy principles and significators

Planet / luminary	Energy principle	Esoteric refinement	Orthodox significator of:	Esoteric significator of:
Sun*	Vitality	There are three kinds of vitality: i) Fire by friction ii) Solar Fire iii) Electric Fire (see above, The Veils)	Identity	Present identity; assemblage point of consciousness in present lifetime, the quality of which will be determined by which of the three kinds of fire the Sun represents
Moon	Continuity & Perpetuation	Continuity provided by: i) etheric body ii) astral body iii) causal body	Emotional nature	Quality of past life consciousness / physical vehicle
Mercury	Communication	Most important is the communication between soul & personality	Perception & communication	The word/ speech/ lower mind
Venus	Attraction	The attraction is mental attraction i.e. that of like for like; the attraction of opposites is a condition belonging to lower level	Quality of loving / values	Mind / the mental body
Mars	Assertion	Desire is the motive for assertion	Quality & focus of effort	Desire / the astral body
Jupiter	Expansiveness /	The means of a	Area of life /	Attainment

		inclusion	more inclusive consciousness	psyche where there is least restriction	through reaching out
Saturn	Restriction / challenge	Limitation is a mental condition;	Area of life / psyche in which there is habitual restriction	The dominant & conditioning thought form over lifetimes
Uranus	Liberation	The liberation of the lower by the higher	Intuition	Intuition / soul contact on the mental plane
Neptune	Unification	Achieved on the astral plane by the merging of the separated reality into a higher reality	Transcendence	The Presence / the soul sensed on the astral plane
Pluto	Destruction	Achieved by dragging hindering factors out of the unconscious and destroying	Transformation	The cleansing agent of the soul, active in the lower nature
Vulcan	Re-construction	Achieved from the destruction of what formerly existed	-	The agent of regeneration, active in the etheric vehicle
The Earth	Strength through struggle	-	-	The sustainer
Chiron	Recovery	Achieved by means of spiritual crisis	The scar on the soul	The cornerstone of the spiritual identity

* Please note that the sun is technically a star and not a planet, and as such it is representative of a higher order than that of the planets.

Planets and Decanates

Again, this information has been given elsewhere, but we are presenting it, below, with the emphasis upon the planet.

Planet	Ray	1st decanate of:	2nd decanate of:	3rd decanate of:
Sun	II	Leo	Aries & Scorpio	Gemini, Sagittarius & Capricorn
Moon	IV	Taurus (with Venus)	Pisces	Cancer
Mercury	IV	Virgo	Taurus, Cancer & Aquarius	Libra
Venus	V	Taurus (with the Moon)	Capricorn	Virgo, Scorpio & Aquarius
Mars	VI	Scorpio	Sagittarius	Aries, Leo & Pisces
Jupiter	II	Aries, Libra, Sagittarius & Pisces	Leo	-
Saturn	III	Capricorn	Virgo & Libra	Taurus

The Rays and Decanates (via the planetary rulers)

Collected and represented, the above table gives us the following

Sign	1st decanate expresses:	2nd decanate expresses:	3rd decanate expresses:
Aries	II	II / VII *	VI
Taurus	IV or V	IV	III
Gemini	II	VI	II / VI *
Cancer	V	IV	IV/ VII *
Leo	II	II	VI
Virgo	IV	III	V
Libra	II	III	IV
Scorpio	VI	II / VI*	V
Sagittarius	II	VI	II/VI*
Capricorn	III	V	II /VII*
Aquarius	III	IV	V
Pisces	II	IV/ VI*	VI

*denotes fluid

Categorising by Theme: The Aspects

To assist the matter of esoteric interpretation, it is of value to use the idea of the three aspects to create three categories.

The first aspect is the concern of orthodox astrology. It is concerned with the down-flowing of force, with form, and with the experience upon the mutable cross. The emphasis is upon personality and not soul.

- There is likely to be a predominance of planets in the first decanate of the signs or a mix of planets in the first and second decanates. In such cases, stick to the techniques of conventional astrology, using the traditional rulers and introducing esoteric considerations circumspectly.
- The Sun represents the energy of fire by friction.
- The Moon will be a veil for Vulcan, the ruler of the etheric body. This indicates that the assemblage point of past life and the foundation of consciousness is the physical body.

The second aspect is the prime concern of esoteric astrology. It is concerned with the transformation of energy and the experience on the fixed cross. The soul is now active within the form.

- The planets in the second decanate will be in the majority. In such cases, use the esoteric rulers to analyse the quality of the life. Charts of this kind will be very common among those coming forward for esoteric astrological readings.
- The Sun will be a veil for Neptune and will represent the energy of solar fire.
- The Moon will also veil Neptune, the ruler of the astral body. This indicates that the assemblage point of past life was the emotions and the foundation of the consciousness is the astral body.

The third aspect is the stage at which the will is being developed upon the cardinal cross. From this point, the horoscope is a dispensable and frequently unreliable guide as the will, expressing itself through the zodiacal signs, will be strong enough to overrule planetary influence.

- The third decanate of the signs is emphasised. In such cases, use the esoteric rulers to analyse the quality of the life and the hierarchical rulers of third decanate planets to see how the Initiate's being is linked into other planes of the solar system.
- The Sun will be a veil for Uranus and represent the energy of electric fire.
- The Moon will be a veil for Uranus, the ruler of the causal body. This indicates that the assemblage point of past life and the foundation of consciousness is the mental body. Expect examples of charts of this kind to be few.

Planetary Exaltations

The planetary exaltations is one of a number of concepts that is in danger of being lost to conventional astrology as computerisation enables corners to be cut.

Certain signs enable the luminaries and the inner and superior planets to give their *optimum* expression. In the sign that is its polar opposite, the planet gives a very weak, debilitated expression and is said to be in its fall.

Esoteric astrology has not developed its own system of exaltations (see Endnote 2), but borrows that of orthodox astrology, identifying:

- Planets in their exaltation as strong planets, the energy, allegiances, and significance of which will dominate the chart and the lifetime
- Planets in their fall indicate planetary energies that are in the process of being held down

Both conditions have implications for development, and this concept may prove particularly useful when used in conjunction with the crosses of the heavens (see Chapter 4).

Planet	Exaltation	Fall
Sun	Aries	Libra
Moon	Taurus	Scorpio
Mercury	Virgo	Pisces
Venus	Pisces	Virgo
Mars	Capricorn	Cancer
Jupiter	Cancer	Capricorn
Saturn	Libra	Aries

Planetary Dispositors

Perhaps because it is less concerned with prediction, Western astrology makes less of dispositors than Hindu astrology, in which discipline dispositors and the blending of energies created by the dispositing situation is the basis of the predictive craft. Dispositors are a profoundly useful tool to the esoteric astrologer, precisely because they enable refinement through blending.

Let us define a dispositor:

♦ A dispositor is any planet occupying a sign it does not rule. In occupying this sign it is displacing or dispositing the ruler. For example, Mercury in Sagittarius disposits Jupiter, which is the orthodox ruler of the sign Sagittarius.

This dispositing situation creates an immediate link between Mercury (and the houses of the horoscope that it rules) and Jupiter and the houses that Jupiter rules. This blending of energies acts as a conditioning influence upon Mercury and all that it represents in a chart.

This same blending technique may be adopted by the esoteric astrologer, but his dispositing situations are created by the esoteric rulers, thus:

> Any planet in the sign Aries disposits Mercury.
> Any planet in the sign Taurus disposits Vulcan.
> Any planet in the sign Gemini disposits Venus.
> Any planet in the sign Cancer disposits Neptune.*
> Any planet in the sign Leo disposits Neptune.*
> Any planet in the sign Virgo disposits the Moon.**
> Any planet in the sign Libra disposits Uranus.
> Any planet in the sign Scorpio disposits Mars.
> Any planet in the sign Sagittarius disposits the Earth.
> Any planet in the sign Capricorn disposits Saturn.
> Any planet in the sign Aquarius disposits Jupiter.
> Any planet in the sign Pisces disposits Pluto.

*Ruler of the second aspect of the sign.
** Veiling Neptune.

In each of the dispositing situations listed above, the sign ruled esoterically by the dispositing planet is:

- ♦ Blended with that of the sign in which the dispostion takes place.
- ♦ Blended also with that sign in which the disposited planet is located.

This creates a triple blend of considerable significance in describing the conditioning factors at work on any planet and upon that thing which, according to conventional astrology, the planet rules.

By such means, the astrologer links form and quality, which is the central concern of transitional astrology.

Endnotes

1. This statement from *The Secret Doctrine* may be of interest:
   "The seven planetary spirits or angels . . . are identical with the Dyan Chohans of the esoteric doctrine and have been transformed into the archangels and spirits of the presence by the Christian Church."

2. Indeed, there is a case for saying that esoteric astrology has no need, because the exaltations and falls represent an attempt to reveal the essential quality (soul) of the planet, whereas the orthodox system of rulerships and detriments express the personality.

Chapter 6

Looking Again at the Houses

"There are twelve celestial houses in astrology. They are derived from an equal division of the circle of observation into twelve parts. What is this circle of observation? It is an imaginary line passing from the eastern horizon, through the point immediately overhead, through the western horizon, the point immediately beneath our feet, round to the eastern horizon again. In astronomy, this is called the vertical of latitude belonging to the place of birth. This circle is called a vertical because it is always vertical to the circle of the horizon. One twelfth part of the circle of observation constitutes an astrological 'house' . . . . All the affairs of life are distributed among the twelve houses."
—Sepharial

"Ina general sense, the signs are said to relate to character, the houses to environment."
—Charles Carter

"The houses are the prison of the soul."
—D.K.

It is sometimes forgotten that astrology is only as good as the questions to which its language is applied. Astrology, of itself, actually says nothing, but it can be made to say much. This consideration needs to be to the fore when looking again at the houses that personalise celestial influences and provide the very structure for horoscopy.

The houses exist as central pillars of exoteric predictive astrology that has been out of fashion in the West for the past thirty years; in the hands of a Hindu astrologer, the houses can be made to disclose down to the level of the number of cattle owned and the colour of a front door. To someone who knows how to read a natal chart in such a way, the houses also show the physical vehicle at both the dense physical and subtle levels: They show the condition of the frame, organs, glands, and chakras. In more psychologically oriented astrology, they represent areas within the psyche that give the personality its definition. For esoteric astrologers, they unfold life's experiences and developmental stages.

The houses show us all levels of personal reality. It is up to us as astrologers to make them yield the kind of information we want from them, and as it is the job of the esoterically inclined astrologer to help a client to find his path, we must make the houses help us in this task.

The astrologer who disdains to involve himself with the techniques of analysing form is probably missing the point of incarnation on planet Earth. We live in a world of form, and even if we wish it otherwise, most of us throughout the course of our lives are affected deeply, at one level or another, by events. If we know how to read them, we can uncover ourselves in the events we draw to ourselves.

The personality creates its own environment; life and time grant the opportunity to experience that creation, and horoscopy gives us a way of understanding it.

The spiritual path begins in our own backyards, amid the clutter of the personality and often in the places we will not think to look if we have set our sights too high or are too abstract in our thinking about spiritual development.

It is the job of the spiritually oriented astrologer to offer the refinements and to explain why it is happening and the point of it all. Esoteric understanding can help here, but unless we are prepared to build a bridge between everyday life and our spiritual aspirations, the discipline of esoteric astrology will remain remote and hanging in space, rather as the Earth appears to the fallen angels of Milton's *Paradise Lost*.

By way of concluding this introduction, let us remind ourselves of the context:
♦ The planets (World Five) distribute to the world of bodies (World Seven) that return it in the form of consciousness to planetary life (World Six).

The houses surround the individual members of the human family in World Seven, determining how they receive and how they return energy. The houses, like the zodiacal signs of which they are a lower correspondence, are a product of human thinking over the ages about the experience of living (see Endnote 1). They have their own conditioning power. The houses are derived from the Earth's diurnal motion on its axis and represent the lowest expression of the lesser zodiac.

The houses and the twelve areas of life experience

First House
House of Aries; natural ruler: Mars
Awareness through self-assertion and personal effectiveness

Persona—self-image—physical appearance—brain—head and face

Second House
House of Taurus; natural ruler: Venus
Awareness through acquisition and material consolidation
Values—personal resources—money and possessions—the throat—thyroid gland—throat chakra

---

Third House
House of Gemini; natural ruler: Mercury Awareness through communication

The rational mind—the separated reality—the written and spoken word—education and places of learning—the environment—the siblings—the hands, arms, and shoulders—the thymus gland (third aspect of the heart centre triad)

Fourth House
House of Cancer; natural ruler: Moon
Awareness through the experience of perpetuation and continuity
Link to the astral plane: collective unconscious—the personal past—the childhood—the mother and motherhood—the home—real estate—the breasts and upper stomach

---

Fifth House
House of Leo; natural ruler: Sun
Awareness through the expression of creativity
Individuality—creativity—conception of children—recreation—the health (second aspect of the heart centre triad)

Sixth House
House of Virgo; natural ruler: Mercury
Awareness through the expression of function and execution of duty
Work—vocation—health—domestic pets—lower stomach—pancreas—the solar plexus (first aspect of the heart centre triad)

Seventh House
House of Libra; natural ruler: Venus
Awareness through experience in personal relationships
Relationship—balance—partnerships with commitment—kidneys—the adrenal glands—the base chakra

---

Eighth House
House of Scorpio; natural ruler: Mars/Pluto
Awareness through losing self in other
Sympathy—death—sexual union—shared resources—reproductive organs and bowels—the sacral chakra—the gonads

---

Ninth House
House of Sagittarius; natural ruler: Jupiter Awareness through the search for meaning
Higher knowledge—religion and law—other countries and cultures—overseas travel—the hips and thighs—the spleen

Tenth House
House of Capricorn; natural ruler: Saturn Awareness though working for recognition
Authority—the establishment—the father—the career—the knees—carotid gland—alta major
centre (first aspect of the head centre triad)

Eleventh House
House of Aquarius; natural ruler: Saturn/Uranus Awareness through fellowship and communal
endeavour
Ideals—fellowship—communal activities—groups—children after birth (the next generation)—
the calves and ankles—the pituitary gland (second aspect of the head centre triad)

Twelfth House
House of Pisces; natural ruler: Jupiter/Neptune Awareness through the experience of non-separation
Compassion—self transcendence—restriction—seclusion—the feet—the pineal gland (third
Aspect of the head centre triad)

Working through a house, a planet will bring experiences of a kind that will be shaped by the
house involved. Whatever the house, whatever its emphasis, the esoterically inclined astrologer
must accept *unconditionally* that experiences in this area of life are as spiritually valid and useful
as any other. It is not the astrologer's place to make judgements about which houses are more or
less "spiritual"; indeed, there is *no* distinction to be made because they all represent valid aspects
of the one life. The astrologer is, rather, to use understanding of the function of the planets to
ascertain which areas of life contain the way forward, and which represent the old way of being.
This is an entirely individual matter (see Endnote 2).

Working with The Houses

The houses, like the signs to which they correspond, can be categorised by element and by quality.
The idea of polarity can also be transposed to the level of the houses to good effect, as can the
tripartite division which gives us the decanates. There are astrologers who attribute considerable
significance to the position of the planet within the house (ie, is at the beginning, close to the
cusp, the middle or the end.) We ourselves are of the view that if the aim is to analyse form with
precision, the twelve houses, collectively, need to yield twenty-eight subdivisions that correspond
to the lunar mansions, because the Moon rules form (see Endnote 3). This kind of knowledge
belongs to exoteric astrology.

Astrologers with a spiritual orientation must use as many of these techniques as they find useful,
bearing in mind that they are likely to be approached by clients who view their problems as
arising in the world out there, rather than in their own energy fields and consciousness. To
focus on consciousness to the exclusion of form is to run a strong risk of losing your client, both
intellectually and emotionally.

There is one consideration which is of fundamental importance to astrologers of all hues and that is the relative strength of the signs and the houses.

Students struggling to master conventional astrological interpretation frequently ask the question: To which should precedence be given: a planet's house placement or the sign in which it is found? The answer is, unequivocally, the house placement (see Endnote 4).
Esoterically oriented students need to be aware of this, too.

In undeveloped man and disciples, the planet's house placement dominates and the sign adds refinement. Only in the charts of initiates do the houses together with planetary influences themselves begin to fade out. This point has been made already in earlier chapters, but it bears repeating. The matter of precedence has significance for the determination of the two principal rays: the egoic (or soul) ray and the personality ray.

The houses and the planes of consciousness

The houses that correspond to the mental plane (upper mental); developing mental substance:
House I: idea of separated self
House V: idea of relating self
House IX: idea of spiritual self

The houses that correspond to the astral plane (see Endnote 5); developing emotional substance:
House II: desire for possessions
House VI: desire for vocation
House X: desire for public recognition and acceptance of personality (and, later, the spiritual self)

The houses that correspond to the intellectual plane (lower mental): developing intellectual substance:
House III: personal reality
House VII: relating reality
House XI: group reality

The synthetic houses: developing the causal body
House IV: synthesising constituent parts of physical self-etheric body (first permanent atom: the physical)
House VIII: synthesising the emotional self-astral body (second permanent atom: the astral)
House XII: synthesising the aspirational self-mental body (third permanent atom: the mental)

These three permanent atoms provide the foundation of the causal body.

In effect, these categories enable an astrologer to map the subtle anatomy, the place where spiritual crises and illness arise. The implications of this for diagnosis, healing, and spiritual guidance are considerable. Students are encouraged to become familiar with them and to get working with them as soon as possible.

The Areas of Consciousness

As stated in the introduction to this chapter, it is the responsibility of the astrologer to ensure that he categorises the houses in ways which are useful to him and the client. It was with this in mind that, during the early 1990s, we developed the concept of the areas of consciousness. It was felt that this grouping of the houses represented a useful halfway house between conventional astrology and esoteric astrology: The concept of the areas of consciousness belongs, quintessentially, to transitional astrology.

This concept is based upon the law of three and enshrines the esoteric idea that:
$$lst + 2nd + 3rd = \textbf{4th}$$
(three constituents combine to make a fourth entity)

Thus:

First Houses I + II + III = House IV Houses of Personal Consciousness
+
Second Houses V+ VI+ VII = House VIII Houses of Relating Consciousness
+
Third Houses IX + X + XI = House XII Houses of Universal Consciousness

Fourth Houses IV + VIII + XII = Egoic Consciousness

All houses in all three areas of consciousness should be understood as conferring opportunities of a certain kind which, in turn, will develop consciousness of a certain quality.

The Houses of Personal Consciousness: Building a personal reality

Experience: the development of personal capacity and discovery of self. Collectively, these houses represent the first aspect, life.
- ♦ They are concerned with outgoingness and the taking on of form.
- ♦ Their focus is the development of an awareness of the separated self.
- ♦ They correspond to the mutable cross that governs the descent into matter and the amassing of experience.

House I: The opportunity to assert self and for leaving one's mark upon the world. This develops awareness of the ability to do. The sign describes the mode of self-assertion.
House II: The opportunity to pursue and acquire that which is of value. This develops motivation and determination. The sign describes the quality of those things to which value is given.
House III: The opportunity is to communicate and use ideas to build a personal reality. This develops intellectual capacity. The sign(s) involved describes the quality of the personal reality.
House IV: In this house, there is the opportunity to become self-conscious through awareness of that which dwells within the form. The sign describes the quality of the consciousness.

The Houses of Relating Consciousness: Building awareness of self and other

Experience: engaging with different realities

Collectively, these houses represent the second aspect, quality.
- They are concerned with the development of consciousness within the form.
- Their focus is the interaction between self and other and the definition provided by contrast and comparison.
- They correspond to the fixed cross which governs the emergence of soul consciousness.

House V: The opportunity is to express self creatively and to gain confirmation of personal value from others. This develops awareness of individuality. The sign describes the nature of the creative expression.

House VI: The opportunity is to use resources, both physical and emotional, in the service of others. This develops commitment and responsibility to others. The sign describes the nature of the service to be rendered.

House VII: The opportunity is to learn about one's true qualities from the experience of interacting with and projecting onto others. This develops awareness of accountability.
The sign describes the qualities that a person will *come* to manifest as a result of his associations.

House VIII: In this house, there is the opportunity to come to consciousness about self in relation to others. Through challenge, a person discovers, in the context of his own life and his dealings with others, what is true and what is false and what is right and what is wrong.

The Houses of Universal Consciousness: Building awareness of soul consciousness

Experience: The development of a sense of purposefulness.

Collectively, these houses represent the third aspect, appearance (or manifestation), which is the blend of life, a quality of consciousness and purpose, intelligently conceived.
- They are concerned with the development of group consciousness.
- Their focus is the point of interface between the individual and the group and the ending of separation.
- They correspond to the cardinal cross which governs the emergence of spiritual will.

House IX: The opportunity is to search for the larger context which gives purpose to the individual. This develops a spiritual perspective. The sign describes the nature of the quest.

House X: The opportunity is to gain recognition and status through self-advancement. This develops a sense of public responsibility. The sign describes the nature of the aspirations.

House XI: The opportunity is to find a role for oneself in the group and to become active as a force for change. This develops group consciousness. The sign describes the nature and purpose of the affiliations.

House XII: The opportunity is to lose the restricting effects of a reality rooted in separation. This develops soul consciousness. The sign describes the way in which a person will merge with others.

It is emphasised that neither the houses nor the areas of consciousness, of themselves, are any guide to the level of development. For example, a personality can be working in the area of personal consciousness in order to develop, refine, or perfect, as an undeveloped man, as a disciple or as an initiate. In each case, however, the quality of the response given to the experiences offered by the houses will be different. The houses are to be understood as places of learning: They are, in effect, the loom of consciousness.

The planets in the areas of consciousness

The planets may usefully be placed in one of three categories:

The inner planets: Attraction into an area of life/consciousness
i.   The Sun, Mercury, Vulcan, and Venus
ii.   The Earth and Mars
iii. The Moon
The superior planets: Consolidation within an area of life/consciousness Jupiter and Saturn
The outer planets: Withdrawal from an area of life/consciousness
i.   Uranus, Neptune, and Pluto
ii.   Chiron

The Inner Planets

i.   These planets will always be bunched together. Venus, which is the farthest away from the Sun, will never make an aspect exceeding sixty degrees (the equivalent of two houses). The emphasis provided by the intimate planets indicates the areas of life/consciousness to which a person is attracted and in which he is to engage consciously. The sun forms the epicentre.

ii.   Mars can be a considerable distance away from the sun, and the Earth, of necessity, is in the polar opposite degree to the Sun. The houses in which each is found are areas of importance in the life: Mars, in an obvious way, identifying the field of expression, and the Earth, in a more subtle way, indicating the area of life upon which a person draws constantly as he attempts to function in the areas of life marked out by the intimate planets.

iii. The Moon indicates the area of life/consciousness that has provided the assemblage point for the inherited (a priori) sense of self.

The Superior Planets

The house occupied by Jupiter indicates the area of life/consciousness in which a person demonstrates expansiveness and experiences the benevolence of deity. Saturn, by contrast, indicates the area of life in which the mind has been contained for many lifetimes. It is a place of restriction and such close identification that a person may not be aware of his Saturnian perspectives. For him, they condition life itself.

The Outer Planets

i.   Wherever the outer planets appear in the chart, in those areas of life, there is withdrawal of the personality. Uranus, the agent of the soul, liberates in which ever house it is found; Neptune blurs the distinctions upon which depend the integrity of the separated self; and Pluto exposes and destroys the hidden causes of attachment.

ii. Chiron indicates the area of life/consciousness that is the scene of spiritual tension but which, eventually, will become the cornerstone of the spiritual identity.

Another consideration of importance are the respective positions of the ruling planets, both orthodox and esoteric and the orthodox ruler of the sun sign, which is the key to personality ray.

We will return to these interpretations of the roles of the planets as we examine the principal concepts and the principal tools of transitional astrology.

Endnotes

1. It is believed that the concept of the houses was introduced to astrology, along with the concept of individuality, by the Greeks.

2. So much contemporary astrological thinking is flawed, not simply by astrological clichés, but also by spiritual clichés. The spiritual cliché presents Pisces and the psychically sensitive water signs as having spiritual potential, and Aries, the earth signs and the second house as being in some way lacking in spirituality. In terms of esoteric understanding, this is profoundly inadequate, and in terms of the message, it conveys to the client or seeker is equally unhelpful.

3. The degrees of the cusps of the lunar mansions are as follows:

Aries:—Libra 0 degrees
Aries—Libra 12 $^6/7$ degrees
Aries—Libra 25 $^5/7$ degrees
Taurus—Scorpio 8 $^4/7$ degrees
Taurus—Scorpio 21 $^3/7$ degrees
Gemini—Sagittarius 4 $^2/7$ degrees
Gemini—Sagittarius 17 $^1/7$ degrees
Cancer—Capricorn 0 degrees
Cancer—Capricorn 12 $^6/7$ degrees
Cancer—Capricorn 25 $^5/7$ degrees
Leo—Aquarius 8 $^4/7$ degrees
Leo—Aquarius 21 $^3/7$ degrees
Virgo—Pisces 4 $^2/7$ degrees
Virgo—Pisces 17 $^1/7$ degrees

4. Few contemporary astrology text books deal with this matter. This may well be because many have been written by theoretical astrologers who may not have had a great deal of practical experience.

5. These houses may be ruled by Earth signs, but they correspond to the astral plane. Think this through (astral reversal is a factor), and try giving an astral overlay to your understanding of the dynamics of these houses. It will add an important dimension: that of desire. Although this may not add much to your understanding of House II, it may make quite a difference in respect of Houses VI and X. People with inner planets in these houses are driven to serve or to gain public recognition.

Part Two: Supplement

The esoteric significance of the zodiacal signs

Aries
In conventional astrology:

Element: Fire
Quality: Cardinal
Natural ruler of the First House: *Self-assertion*

In esoteric astrology:

One arm of the cardinal cross

Ruler of the Creative Hierarchy on fourth ray which is out of manifestation but active on the cosmic astral plane and expressing the principle of unity through effort.

Transmits first and seventh rays into our system.

Orthodox ruler: Mars (sixth ray) Esoteric ruler: Mercury (fourth ray)
Hierarchical ruler: Uranus (first and seventh rays)

Rules: Beginnings, including that created by the crisis of reversal, but to admit the new, it has to destroy the old. It is therefore a sign of death, as well as birth.

The keynotes of the sign Aries:
- ♦ expresses the will to be and do
- ♦ unfolds the power to manifest
- ♦ enters into battle for the Lord
- ♦ strives for unity through effort

Key quotations from *Esoteric Astrology:*
- ♦ "Aries governs the path of discipleship. The Will to Return to the Source. Determination to achieve liberation. The emanating cause of the changes upon the Mutable and Fixed Crosses."
- ♦ "Aries [is] the birthplace of Divine Ideas whether these ideas are souls brought into incarnation . . . or whether they are the birth of the

ideas of God in the form of hierarchical plans to which the Initiate becomes sensitive."

♦ "In Aries, we have the duality which is attached to the bringing together of spirit and matter in the great creative activity of manifestation at the beginning of the evolutionary cycle."

♦ "In its lowest manifestation, Aries is the creator of those activities, conditions and processes which lead to the manifestation of soul through the medium of form, and later those higher undertakings which lead in due time to the manifestation of spirit through soul."

Decanates ruled by first Jupiter, second Sun, and third Mars

Taurus
In orthodox astrology:

Element: Earth
Quality: Fixed
Natural ruler of the second house—Values

In esoteric astrology:

One arm of the fixed cross

Ruler of the Creative Hierarchy on fifth ray, which is out of manifestation, but active on the cosmic astral plane and expressing the principle of light through knowledge.

Transmits fourth ray into our system.

Orthodox ruler: Venus (fifth ray)
Esoteric ruler: Vulcan (first ray)
Hierarchical ruler: Vulcan

Rules: The transmutation of desire into aspiration and illumination.

Keynotes of the sign Taurus:
♦ entrance to the path of discipleship
♦ creates the desire to overcome desire
♦ opens the eye of the bull, which reveals the plan of deity

Key quotations from *Esoteric Astrology:*
♦ "As the individual descends into incarnation and when he takes an astral shell, he definitely comes into a Taurean cycle, for it is desire which impels to rebirth and it takes the potency of Taurus to bring this about."

- ♦ "[This sign is called] 'the sign of major life incentive' because Taurus is the symbol of desire in all its phases."
- ♦ "It was the Buddha who clarified for man the nature of desire and its results, with the unhappy effects which desire produces when persistent and unenlightened."
- ♦ "Taurus—The longing for liberation. The transmutation of desire into Love."

Decanates ruled by first Venus or Moon, second Mercury, and third Saturn

---

Gemini
In orthodox astrology:

Element: Air Quality: Mutable
Natural ruler of the third house: Personal reality and communication

---

In esoteric astrology

One arm of the mutable cross

Ruler of the creative hierarchy on the sixth ray which is out of incarnation, but active on the cosmic astral plane and expressing the principle of desire for duality.

Transmits the second ray into our system.

Orthodox ruler: Mercury (fourth ray)
Esoteric ruler: Venus (fifth ray)
Hierarchical ruler: the Earth (third ray)

Rules: The intermediary principle (ie, that which communicates between soul and body and between soul and spirit).

Keynotes of the sign Gemini:
- ♦ related to the etheric body
- ♦ governs attraction and repulsion, which are conditioning factors of solar life
- ♦ brings about the fusion of opposites
- ♦ the force which is needed for the evolution of Christ consciousness at any particular point in time and space

Key quotations from *Esoteric Astrology:*
- ♦ "All souls, as individual entities . . . [emerge] . . . as vital entities in the sign Gemini."
- ♦ "In the average person, the etheric vehicle is the transmitter of psychic energy, galvanising and co-ordinating the dense physical body and

permitting, therefore, astral and mental control of the personality . . . When the man is upon the path of discipleship and therefore upon the reversed wheel, leading to initiation, the etheric body becomes the transmitter of soul energy and not personality force."

♦ "Through the activity of Mercury, the man whose sun is in Gemini is aided to attain the synthesis of soul and form; through the activity of Jupiter, the man whose rising sign is in Gemini is enabled to attain the consciousness and integration of spirit."

♦ "The cosmic line of force from Gemini to Sagittarius and the reverse is subjectively and esoterically related to our Earth, thus guaranteeing its soul development, the unfoldment of form as an expression of that soul, and leading our sorrowful humanity upon this woeful planet inevitably to the very gate of initiation in Capricorn."

> Decanates ruled by first Jupiter, second Mars, and third the Sun

---

Cancer

In orthodox astrology:

Element: Water
Quality: Cardinal
Natural Ruler of the Fourth House: Continuity and *perpetuation*

In esoteric astrology:

Ruler of the Creative Hierarchy on seventh ray, which is on the verge of liberation from the cosmic physical plane and which expresses the principle of mass life.

Transmits third and seventh rays into our system.

Orthodox ruler: Moon (fourth ray)
Esoteric ruler: Neptune (sixth ray)
Hierarchical ruler: Neptune

Rules: The sustaining principle (ie, the past as sustainer of the present and mass life as sustainer of the individual).

Keynotes of the sign Cancer:
♦ meeting place of form and the feeling-sensitive nature
♦ confers instinctual awareness
♦ junction of the past and present
♦ emergence of individual consciousness from mass consciousness by which the individual is sustained

Key quotations from *Esoteric Astrology:*

- ♦ "All souls come into incarnation in the sign Cancer."
- ♦ "[The sign Cancer is] the doorway into life of those who must know death."
- ♦ "Cancer . . . [is ruled] . . . by only one planet, though in orthodox astrology the Moon is substituted for Neptune because it is the form nature which is dominant in the longest stage of human unfoldment, just as esoterically, it is the feeling-sensitive nature which dominates the average man; it is with this unstable tendency that the disciple has to wrestle."
- ♦ "Even at a relatively high point of development and upon the returning wheel . . . [this sign] . . . preserves ever the mass relationship for the benefit of the incarnating individual and in order to guarantee the ultimate salvation of substance itself."

Decanates ruled by first Venus, second Mercury, and third Moon

---

Leo
In orthodox astrology:

Element: Fire
Quality: Fixed
Natural ruler of the fifth house: Individuality and creativity

---

In esoteric astrology:

One arm of the fixed cross

Ruler of the creative hierarchy known as the divine flames. Operative on the first plane of our solar system. The energy of this hierarchy is called parashakti, or supreme energy.

Transmits first ray into our system.

Orthodox ruler: Sun (second ray)
Esoteric ruler: Sun
Hierarchical ruler: Sun

Rules: The emergence of soul consciousness in the individual.

Keynotes of the sign Leo:

- ♦ the birthplace of the individual
- ♦ the self-centred man eventually becomes the soul in life
- ♦ expression
- ♦ the sign in which a man prepares for the first initiation (integration of the physical and astral)

♦ the sign in which human personality achieves the highest of which it is capable

Key quotations from *Esoteric Astrology:*
  ♦ "[The sign Leo marks] . . . the coming into form of individual self conscious man who emerges out of the mass and herd in Cancer, substituting, for instinctual consciousness, self-awareness and a sense of responsibility of an individual kind."
  ♦ "Leo is the sign where the individual is developed and utilised and finally consecrated to divine purpose. It is related to Polaris the pole Star and is also particularly susceptible to the influence of the Pointer in the Great Bear which is nearest the Pole Star. Esoterically speaking, the Pole Star is regarded as a 'star of orientation' whereby the art of retracing and recovering that which is lost is developed. This eventually brings a man back to his original source."
  ♦ "The Sons of Mind, the self-conscious sons of God, are above everything else, the Sons of Fire, for 'Our God is a consuming Fire.'"
  ♦ "The sign [Leo] . . . has frequently been described as the battlefield of the forces of Materialism and the forces of Light."

Decanates ruled by first Sun, second Jupiter, and third Mars.

Virgo
In orthodox astrology:

Element: Earth
Quality: Mutable
Natural ruler of the sixth house: Vocation and service

In esoteric astrology:

One arm of the mutable cross

Ruler of the creative hierarchy called the divine builders. Operative on the second plane of our solar system, the energy of this hierarchy is Kriyashakti, or materialising ideal.

Transmits second ray into our system.

Orthodox ruler: Mercury (fourth ray)
Esoteric ruler: Moon (fourth ray)
Hierarchical ruler: Jupiter (second ray)

Rules: The nurturing of Christ consciousness

Keynotes of the sign Virgo:
- ♦ the cosmic mother (ie, the negative pole to positive spirit)
- ♦ in the service of the present
- ♦ nurtures the developing soul
- ♦ blends soul and body

Key quotations from *Esoteric Astrology:*
- ♦ "[The] symbology [of Virgo] . . . concerns the whole goal of the evolutionary process which is to shield, nurture and finally reveal the hidden spiritual reality."
- ♦ "Gemini and Virgo are closely related but Gemini presents the pairs of opposites—soul and body—as two separate entities whereas in Virgo they are blended and of supreme importance to each other; the mother protects the germ of the Christ life; matter guards and nurtures the hidden soul."
- ♦ "Virgo is . . . the opposite pole of spirit and stands for the relation of the two after they have been brought together originally in Aries and have produced a recognised duality in Gemini."
- ♦ "It has been said that Virgo 'involves the service of the immediate present,' or in other words, that God immanent evokes a reaction from the form side of life and is thereby served."

Decanates ruled by first Mercury, second Saturn, and third Venus

---

Libra
In orthodox astrology:

Element: Air
Quality: Cardinal
Natural ruler of the seventh house: Self and other

In esoteric astrology:

One arm of the cardinal cross

Ruler of the creative hierarchy called the lesser builders. Operative on the third plane of our solar system, the energy of this hierarchy is Jnanashakti, or force of mind.

Transmits third ray into our system.

Orthodox ruler: Venus (fifth ray)
Esoteric ruler: Uranus (seventh ray)
Hierarchical ruler: Saturn (third ray)

Rules: The attainment of equilibrium between spiritual man and personal man

Keynotes of the sign Libra:

- involved in uncovering the laws according to which God's plan is unfolding
- the sign in which weighing and balancing occurs
- associated with the problem of sex because of the need to find the balance between pairs of opposites
- the decisions reached under this sign in any lifetime will determine the nature of the next

Key quotations from *Esoteric Astrology:*

- "In the days before Leo-Virgo were divided into two signs, Libra was literally the mid-way point."
- "It is in Libra that the balancing of pairs of opposites must take place and reach solution through the judicial mind and the establishment of a point of equilibrium between the male and female principles."
- "Libra—the balancing of desire. The opposite objective to desire is the scales or balances."
- "The emphasis . . . on Gemini and Libra as far as humanity is concerned is on human attainment and achieving the point of balance before other attainments become possible."

Decanates ruled by first Jupiter, second Saturn, and third Mercury.

Scorpio
In orthodox astrology:

Element: Water
Quality: Fixed
Natural ruler of the eighth house: Emotional regeneration

In esoteric astrology:

One arm of the fixed cross

Ruler of the creative hierarchy called the human hierarchy. Operative on the fourth plane of our solar system, the energy of this hierarchy is Mantrikashakti, or the word made flesh.

Transmits fourth ray into our system

Orthodox ruler: Mars (sixth ray)
Esoteric ruler: Mars
Hierarchical ruler: Mercury (fourth ray)

Rules: The establishing of right relations with the soul and with the environment

Keynotes of the sign Scorpio:

- ♦ the sign in which a man is tested; in this sign a man deals with memory and that product of memory, the dweller on the threshold (see Endnote 1)
- ♦ the sign of sex and regeneration
- ♦ the sign of the death of the personality with its longings, desires, ambitions, and pride

Key quotations from *Esoteric Astrology:*

- ♦ "The keynotes of this sign are . . . test, trial and triumph."
- ♦ "Scorpio is under the influence or inflowing energy of Sirius. This is a great star of initiation because our hierarchy (an expression of the second aspect of divinity) is under the supervision or magnetic control of the hierarchy of Sirius."
- ♦ "In this sign, the disciple undergoes those tests which will enable him to take the second initiation and demonstrate that the desire nature is subdued and conquered and that the lower nature is (by being lifted up into the air [ie, into heaven]) capable of reaching the goal for this world period."
- ♦ "The tests of Scorpio are necessarily three in nature as they concern intimately the readiness of the threefold personality:
  1). To reorient itself to the life of the soul and later
  2). To evidence readiness for initiation
  3). To demonstrate sensitivity to the plan thus becoming the one-pointed disciple in Sagittarius."

Decanates ruled by first Mars, second Jupiter, and third moon.

Sagittarius

In orthodox astrology:

Element: Fire
Quality: Mutable
Natural ruler of the ninth house: Seeking union

In esoteric astrology:

One arm of the mutable cross

Ruler of the creative hierarchy called the lunar lords. Operative on the sixth plane of our solar system, the energy of this hierarchy is Kundalinishakti, or energy of matter.

Transmits fourth, fifth, and sixth rays into our system.

Orthodox ruler: Jupiter (second ray)

Esoteric ruler: The Earth (third ray)
Hierarchical ruler: Mars (sixth ray)

Rules: The emergence of the one-pointedness of spiritual man.

Keynotes of the sign Sagittarius:
- ♦ Develops the intuition.
- ♦ In this sign, the disciple learns the importance of goals and commitment to a higher objectives.
- ♦ Awareness of the fifth kingdom in nature (kingdom of souls) replaces identification with the human personality and the human kingdom.
- ♦ A man withdraws completely, in a personality sense, from the form side of life.

Key quotations from *Esoteric Astrology:*
- ♦ "A study of the human family will reveal that every time the man finds himself under the influence of Sagittarius, it is with the objective of orienting himself to some new and higher objective, with the task of refocusing himself towards a higher goal and with the unfoldment of some basic and directing purpose."
- ♦ "In Sagittarius, the intellect which has been developed, used, and finally illumined, becomes sensitive to a still higher type of mental experience and to this we give the name of intuitive perception."
- ♦ "Sagittarius marks . . . a point of balance which follows after . . . [the strenuous testing and trial of Scorpio] . . . for the Archer has to acquire and hold a steady eye, hand and stance prior to firing the arrow which, when directed and correctly followed, will carry him through the portal of initiation."

Decanates ruled by first Jupiter, second Mars, and third Sun.

Capricorn
In orthodox astrology:

Element: Earth\
Quality: Cardinal
Natural ruler of the tenth house: Fusion of personality, ambition, and non-personal goals

In esoteric astrology:

One arm of the cardinal cross

Ruler of the creative hierarchy called the human personality. Operative on the fifth plane of our solar system, the energy of this hierarchy is lchchhashakti, or will to manifest.

Transmits first, third, and seventh rays into our system.

Orthodox ruler: Saturn (third ray)
Esoteric ruler: Saturn
Hierarchical ruler: Venus (fifth ray)

Rules: Initiation and liberation

Keynotes of the sign Capricorn:
- Associated with God, the Holy Spirit.
- Liberation in this sign involves a crystallisation process.
- In this sign, a man reaches either the height of personal ambition or becomes the initiate.
- In this sign, the initiate develops spiritual awareness that is the portal to the higher initiations and is the door out, as Cancer is the door in.

Key Quotations from *Esoteric Astrology:*
- "In Capricorn, the initiate learns to realise the meaning of the growing light which greets his progress as he climbs upwards to the mountain top. The flashes of intuition with which he is becoming familiar change into the blazing and constant light of the soul, irradiating the mind and providing that point of fusion which must ever be the 'fusion of the two lights, the greater and the lesser light.'"
- "Capricorn hides the mystery of God, the Holy Spirit . . . Liberation."
- "[This sign] guards the secret of the soul itself and this is revealed to the initiate at the time of the third initiation. This is sometimes called the 'secret of the hidden glory.'"
- "The doorway into life of those who know not death."

Decanates ruled by first Saturn, second Venus, and third Sun.

Aquarius
In orthodox astrology:

Element: Air
Quality: Fixed
Natural ruler of the eleventh house: Fellows and communal endeavour

---

In esoteric astrology:

One arm of the fixed cross

Ruler of the creative hierarchy called the elemental lives. Operative on the seventh plane of our solar system, this hierarchy embodies no energy principle.

Transmits fifth ray into our solar system

Orthodox ruler: Aquarius (seventh ray)
Esoteric ruler: Jupiter (second ray)
Hierarchical ruler: Moon (fourth ray)

Rules: World service

Keynotes of the sign Aquarius:

♦ In this sign, the service of the personality transmutes itself into the service of humanity.
♦ Selfish and superficial activity gives way to a commitment to be of service to the hierarchy.
♦ Self-consciousness becomes a sensitive humanitarianism.

Key quotations from *Esoteric Astrology:*

♦ "In this sign, the long effort of the soul is consummated and concludes the experience of the disciple upon the fixed cross."
♦ "[It is] . . . a sign in which the significance of cycles is mastered and understood by the initiate. The results of the valley experience (to use the well-known language of mystics of all ages) and of the mountain top with its vision and light are very vividly depicted by the sign. The Aquarian can experience the depths of depression and of self-deprecation or he can pass through the exaltation of the soul and the sense of spiritual power which soul control gives, are known then to be the interplay and the action and reaction which are necessary for growth and comprehension. The Law of such action and reaction is the law with which he works."
♦ "Planetary influences are unusually potent in Aquarius during this world cycle because it is, in a peculiar way, a culminating sign for the majority of people who proceed from Aries to Pisces upon the Fixed Cross . . . [and who then] . . . become liberated world servers . . . joining the ranks of the Hierarchy."
♦ "This constellation is . . . largely responsible for the changes now being effected in our planetary life in all kingdoms of nature, and because it is an air sign, its influence is all-pervasive and interpenetrating."

Decanates ruled by first Saturn, second Mercury, and third Venus

---

Pisces
In orthodox astrology:

Element: Water
Quality: Mutable
Natural ruler of the twelfth house: Unification by absorption

In esoteric astrology:

One arm of the mutable cross

Ruler of the creative hierarchy that is out of manifestation, but active on the cosmic astral plane. The energy of this hierarchy is intelligent substance.

Transmits second and sixth rays into our system.

Orthodox ruler: Jupiter (second ray)
Esoteric ruler: Pluto (first ray)
Hierarchical ruler: Pluto
Rules: The fusion and blending of souls and form.

Keynotes of the sign Pisces:
- This sign gives the experience of bondage or captivity.
- Turns spiritual and mental inhibition into soul expression and mental sensitivity.
- Provokes renunciation or detachment.
- Transforms devotion to the needs of the self into devotion and responsiveness to the needs of humanity.

Key quotations from *Esoteric Astrology:*
- "It is in this dual sign that the imprisoned soul and personality enter upon that process which will transmute the lower nature into the higher manifestation."
- "The ordinary low-grade medium is the outstanding example of the worst aspects of Pisces—negativity, impressionability, animal, and emotional sensitivity with complete underdevelopment of the mental principle."
- "In Pisces, we have the fusion or blending of soul and form as far as man is concerned, producing manifestation of the incarnated Christ, the perfected individual soul, the complete manifestation of the microcosm."
- "Death by drowning or by water in Pisces releases man again into that great centre which we call Humanity, and there experience is gained."

Decanates ruled by first Saturn, second Mercury, and third Venus.

Endnotes

1. In Theosophical writing, the dweller on the threshold is the sum total of all the personality characteristics that have remained unconquered and unsubdued, and have to be finally overcome before initiation can be taken.

Part Three

The Principal Concepts

"An idea is a being incorporeal which has no subsistence by itself but gives figure and form unto shapeless matter and becomes the cause of manifestation."—D.K.

"A warrior cannot complain or regret anything. His life is an endless challenge, and challenges cannot possibly be good or bad. Challenges are simply challenges . . . . The basic difference between an ordinary man and a warrior is that a warrior takes everything as a challenge while an ordinary man takes everything as a blessing or a curse."
Carlos Castaneda
Tales of Power

That thought attracts energy is axiomatic in esotericism.

Concepts are thought forms. They are mental constructs that organise energy, first on the mental level and later on lower levels. All concepts are a form of exclusion, an extrapolation from a potentially limitless pool of possibilities.

After death, what remains of us ourselves are our ideas of ourselves and the concept of ourselves we developed during our lifetimes and which gave coherence and shape to the energies flowing through our personality vehicles. While in incarnation, we can take a view on what we want that to be or we can leave it to default, in which case the concept of ourselves developed in previous lives will impose itself again with just a few changes. But if we organise ourselves mentally, we will develop and eventually ground a new concept of ourselves. All change starts with the idea of change.

The purpose of horoscopy, as we are presenting it here, is to show how we can cooperate in the process of forming of an appropriate and useful concept of self.

Concepts are a means of organising the present and future and of classifying, recognising, and even redeeming what is past. We can and do use concepts unconsciously and without awareness of what they exclude. They are a most potent medium for conditioning.

We can also use concepts consciously, knowing that they will give an emphasis and definition that, in a given situation, will be of value to the realisation of the end in view. This is how an astrologer uses concepts. They enable him to extrapolate from the plethora of detail contained by the natal chart those factors that can be made useful. For the esoteric astrologer the end in view is the effective use of the personality and the opportunity which the lifetime represents. The natal chart guides him through this process.

This chapter is given over to the presentation and explanation of concepts, which will enable an esoterically inclined astrologer to help a client make sense and use of the occurrences in his life. An astrologer's concepts are his antidotes to the reducing effects of conditioning, and they are to be used with conviction. In a reading situation, the energy of certainty can dispel much doubt and despair.

Conditioning

To make sense of our lives, we have to have a way of looking at and understanding our experiences. If we do not consciously use concepts to provide the framework and the categories, conditioning will. The categories provided by conditioning are usually very basic unless they include a strong spiritual component: They reflect the duality in human perception, and life becomes a sequence of pleasant or unpleasant experiences, likes and dislikes, successes and failures, and ups and downs. They are the spokes of the wheel of fortune and the source of untold suffering in untold numbers of us.

Every practising astrologer needs to be aware of conditioning. It lurks in entertaining and seemingly innocuous forms on the pages of magazines and books and in the ideas we swap with each other over the Internet; it exists in the more obvious propagandist forms, which include much radio and television transmission, as well as in our cultural and racial inheritance where it is so difficult to recognise and eradicate. The practising astrologer finds himself engaged in a ceaseless battle against conditioning. It threatens to rob us of authenticity by means of false values and inappropriate expectations and to misread and mishandle the plans revealed by the natal chart.

The defeatism and despair conditioning can create in lives is never more obvious than when, in a reading situation, a client gives a negative reaction to what, after all, is a description of his own potential. It is not uncommon, as you may be aware, to find a person who has had his individuality overlaid by conditioning to the extent that he cannot even recognise himself in an accurate, carefully worded delineation or see further than stereotypical goals. This is to be expected in those who are under the age of twenty-five.

In such a situation, the astrologer can only repeat the salient characteristics in the hope that eventually they will penetrate and there will be resonance. Once this has happened, the situation can move on. The challenge for the astrologer is then to motivate the client to take action to introduce the desired changes in his life. And that has to start with the changes in thinking about the purpose of his life.

At all stages in what is usually a very strenuous process, an astrologer will be helped by a small number of effective concepts designed to counter the effects of conditioning and which will present as purposeful the strife and struggle of existence. This involves letting the idea of challenge replace that of blessings and curses.

Horoscopy will serve the purpose of spiritual development only if it is set to this task by the practitioner. In this chapter, we will be looking at six such concepts, to be used in conjunction with the considerations outlined in the previous chapters and with the techniques to come. These will give the esoterically oriented astrologer the tools of his trade.

The Personality and the Soul

The soul has three aspects: The first is the personality, the vehicle; the second aspect is the ego, the individual human soul; and the third is the monad, or the spiritual soul. In this chapter, we are principally concerned with the second aspect, the ego.

Esoteric astrology is recognised as being the astrology of the soul and, since D.K. opened the doors to this new discipline around the middle of the last century, the idea of it has attracted many people.

Throughout this course, we have pointed out that the astrology of the soul is some way in advance of where most of us are at present. The litmus test here is question: Where do you consider your problems are: in consciousness or in the outside world?

Spiritual ambition may make us want to say "in consciousness," but if we were to ask ourselves that question as our marriages break down, as our children cause us anxiety, and as we face the prospect of redundancy, what is likely to be the honest reply? And how helpful to us then is it to know what ray we are upon? It simply does not provide us with the kind of detail we need if we are to steer ourselves intelligently through such situations, rather than demonstrate passive and stoic acceptance. The soul inhabits a far less complicated world than the personality because there are fewer laws on the higher planes. The personality has to contend with many complications unrecognised by the soul, and there is a practical value in acknowledging this.

The ratio here is 3:7:12. The human soul is governed by nearly twice as many laws as the human Monad and the personality by four times as many.

Through his clients, an esoterically oriented astrologer is likely to encounter a great deal of suffering brought about by unrealistic expectations of self. For example, a person who has made contact with, and has been inspired by a body of spiritual ideas, may be desolated when he discovers that he cannot love unconditionally or that he cannot control his resentment or his anxiety. The unwelcome intrusion of reality that knocks a person off the high place he has attained in his imagination is a common source of spiritual crisis.

To ignore the personality and its agendas is an invitation to trouble. Spiritually, it is useful to acknowledge the personality and get to know it well in order to make it useful to the soul.

Personality-Soul Alignment

The route that all personalities take toward soul consciousness comprises five major stages and involves three initiations:
- emerging from the mass
- experiencing life in all its variety and developing individuality
- refining individuality
- consciously embarking upon the path toward soul consciousness
- alignment

Transitional astrology is the astrology of the aligning personality (ie, the personality that is trying to make itself useful to the soul and which is open to the challenge of transformation). The concepts offered in this chapter reflect those qualities, and they will be of use only to an astrologer who understands that we are here, in personality form, to develop what Gurdjieff called "soul stuff," the causal body that mediates between the spiritual soul on its own plane and the personality.

The Points of Interface

Although Part Four is the place where we will be rounding up the tools an esoterically oriented astrologer will find useful, we give certain details that may be of help in the understanding of these concepts.

- ♦ The Sun, by sign and house position, is the point of interface between the spiritual soul and the personality. It represents potential.
- ♦ The orthodox ruler of the ascendant is the point of interface between the soul (ego) and the personality of the man on the mutable cross.
- ♦ The esoteric ruler of the ascendant is the point of interface between the soul (ego) and the personality of the man on the fixed cross.
- ♦ The cusp of the fifth house is the point of interface between the self-centred personality and the soul-conscious personality.
- ♦ The successful integration and mutual cooperation of the Sun and the esoteric ruler of the ascendant indicates that the personality has achieved alignment and a man is ready to mount the cardinal cross.

The Veils

Nearly all the concepts that follow involve a heavy use of the Sun and Moon. When applying these concepts on natal charts, try to work out which planets the Sun and Moon are veiling because this will greatly affect a person's capacity and orientation.

The sections that follow are significantly shorter than those previous, but they are very dense. Take your time with them, and apply the ideas to your own life and those whose lives you can study by means of their natal charts.

Chapter 7

The Principal Developmental Requirement / Creative Contribution

"Reach for the heavens and hope for the future, for all that
we might be and not just what we are."
The Eagle and the Hawk,
John Denver

"Give and it shall be given unto you is still the truth about life."
—D.H. Lawrence

In this chapter, we look at two concepts that deal with purpose: the purpose of the individual incarnating, expressed in terms of the developmental requirement, and the purpose to which his personal quota of creative energy is to be put.

Both these concepts are concerned with the expression of essence (ie, what truly we are), under the conditioning and beyond the limitations imposed by past-life perceptions. They are concerned with becoming and latent qualities, and for this reason, the astrologer's delineations may not be immediately recognisable to the client. Alternatively, a client may have very strong but non-authentic views on what is his purpose. Both these concepts serve the purposes of spirit, and the energy of spirit is will.

The Principal Developmental Requirement

The principal developmental requirement is to be understood as the transformation of energy in accordance with the karmic requirements. These are shown in the natal chart. The principal developmental requirement represents the soul's intention for the personality that is always to progress the process of achieving alignment.

To understand this concept, it is essential that there is understanding of the transformative process, and an appreciation that all personalities in incarnation have to walk the same route to alignment. This involves five major stages that we defined in the introduction. Equally importantly, however, is the understanding that a person can be at any stage on this route and that an enormously wide range of experiences can provide developmental opportunities. It is not adequate to assume, as so many who have themselves engaged with spirituality do, that only those who have consciously committed to a spiritual path can develop. We can develop without any conscious understanding of spirituality simply by fulfilling the requirements of the life time. By transforming energy, we make our contribution to our planet.

There is a spiritual challenge involved in getting off the Moon sign and giving a confident expression of the energy of the Sun sign. With or without consciousness, such efforts are transformative. D.K. describes this as the line of least resistance for the personality.

Across the soul groups that comprise humanity, there is both a contribution to be made and a balance to be maintained. It can be assumed that each soul group makes its contribution to the collective requirement of humanity and that our energetic composition, as revealed by the natal chart, is fine-tuned by the reincarnating process in order to produce the required yield and maintain the requisite balance. This is why it is said to be difficult to be born. We have to wait for an opportunity.

In Chapter 1, we looked at humanity as an energetic entity, as the synthesising fourth principle, and at humanity's role in regulating the balance between the higher and lower planes. We noted there that of nature's kingdoms, the human is the only kingdom with variable capacity. Humanity's capacity is variable precisely because we have the capacity to develop from average men to supermen, or in more familiar language, from ordinary people to saints and masters.

Development at this level, on the path of evolution, is an integral part of this process of transformation. Our spiritual development matters not only to ourselves but also to our planet, and if we follow the map of our energy circuit, as shown in the accurately cast horoscope, we stand to give our best.

The principal developmental requirement:

Defines: What we are to do in this lifetime (see Endnote 1), the goal of the personality
Principal tool: The Sun by sign and house placement
Context: The energies from World Three are distributed in our solar system by the zodiacal signs (the lower correspondence of the constellations) and within the Earth sphere by Shamballa. The Sun, itself a star and not a planet, is the transformer and distributor of stellar energy within our system.
Astrological significance: Point of interface between the spiritual soul and the personality. It represents the way forward, represents possibility, confers purpose, and develops spiritual will.

Considerations:

- The principal developmental requirement is always expressed in terms of the qualities of the sign. For example, if the Sun is in Taurus, then expressing Taurean qualities and values is purposeful, and represents the way forward. It is progressive to express Taurean attributes and take them into the area of life defined by the house placement of the Sun. The reason for this is to be found in the importance of the Sun as a distributor of stellar energy and its significance within horoscopy.
- The detailed answer to why it should be progressive to do this is found by examining the sign, and particularly the house position, of the

Moon. This symbolises the concept of self in past life. The Sun has the job of opening new possibilities that will involve moving on from this earlier concept of self.

- ♦ The Sun always indicates the way forward, regardless of the signs involved. Should he come across it in a chart, an astrologer caught up in astrological or spiritual clichés may find it hard to understand why, for example, it should be progressive to move onto a sun in Taurus in the second house from a moon in Pisces in twelfth house. The answer, of course, is that it gives a wholly different quality of experience and therefore opens up developmental possibilities of a different kind.

- ♦ The house placement is an ingredient of comparable importance. In this area of life, a person is designed to ground the qualities and values of the Sun sign. This may well be enabling him to make a contribution of a certain kind which has considerable developmental or even karmic significance (see Endnote 2).

- ♦ Be aware that the undertow from the Moon is very strong. Expressing the energy of the Sun sign and house placement represents the line of least resistance for an evolving personality. A personality may be standing still or caught up in repetition (see Endnote 3). The aspect between the Sun and the Moon indicates the extent to which the new direction challenges the old way of being.

- ♦ Saturn will always challenge the Sun that confers new possibilities. Saturn's natural ally is the Moon. Together, they restore the past. To have new experiences, the Sun will need to obtain Saturn's conscious consent (see Chapter 9). If the Sun is in stressful aspect to Saturn in a natal chart, this will prove more difficult to achieve than if the relationship between the two is harmonious.

- ♦ The expression of the values and activities defined by the Sun's placement needs to be integrated with the soul's requirement of the personality as expressed through the ruler of the ascendant.

There is nothing inherently difficult in working with this idea. What is required is a confident and accurate delineation of the Sun sign (see Endnote 4) and the opportunities that this placement opens up for a person interested in spiritual development. In this connection, it is helpful if explanation is offered as to *why* this should represent the way forward.

The planetary ruler of the Sun sign is also an important planet to consider because it describes the way (sign) and area of life (house) in which the values conferred by the Sun sign express themselves. It is also the key to the personality ray.

Creative contribution

Creative contribution is to be understood as the optimum contribution an individual can make.

This concept provides definition in the matter of contribution. The idea that each of us has something to offer is one that needs to be better understood. For too long now, there has been a tendency to view spirituality as a matter of personal salvation and of receiving. In fact, though, spiritually aware people are needed to give out and become agents of transformation in their environments. This concept assumes that each of us has a contribution to make to the tasks that humanity as a whole has to address.

The concept of creative contribution is a supplement to that of the principal developmental requirement. It is underpinned by the idea that individuality and creativity are the reverse sides of the same coin.

Creative contribution:

Defines: The optimum use of the creative energy.
Principal tool: The cusp of the fifth house and the planetary ruler of the fifth house. Context: The sign Leo marks the height of achievement for the human personality (alignment being an achievement of the soul rather than the personality). The personality understands his separateness and individuality, but also appreciates his dependency upon others (see Endnote 5).
This reflects the personality's dependency upon the soul.
Astrological significance: The fifth house is frequently referred to as the house of the soul. It is, of course, the house of Leo and represents the physical organ of the heart. At a higher level, it represents the transforming principle in the heart centre triad which is the seat of the Soul in the personality; the head centre triad when it opens is the seat of the Monad (or Spiritual Soul.)
Considerations: The sign on the cusp of the fifth house describes the quality of the creative capacity; the sign and house position of the orthodox ruler of the fifth house indicates the way and the area of life in which this energy will best express itself.
The house position, sign, and ray of the esoteric ruler of the fifth house will indicate the purpose of the contribution from the point of view of the soul.
Saturn in the fifth house, which blocks the creative expression and interferes with the sense that the individual contribution, could be of any value is likely to provoke spiritual crises.
Be prepared for clients to be uninvolved in, but not uninterested in, the kinds of activities the sign on the cusp of the fifth would indicate as a suitable expression of the creative energy.

Working with This Concept

Again, there is nothing inherently complicated about working with this concept, but it is important when giving guidance about expressing the creative energy to avoid excessive concentration upon form. There is a tendency for spiritually aware people to assume that a valid contribution can

be made only through some specific, spiritually approved activity or artistic form (see Endnote 6).

The following list is offered as guidance in the matter of how to think about the matter of the nature of the creative capacity. It is by no means exhaustive, and students should build their own case histories.

On the cusp of the fifth house	Nature of the creative energy
Aries	Life giving, lends itself to radiatory forms of healing, the martial arts
Taurus	Constructive, expresses itself through naturally occurring materials, particularly wood & clay
Gemini	Communicative, particularly adept with sound and words
Cancer	Nurturing, particularly concerned with children and child welfare and maternity issues
Leo	Performing, particularly drawn to dancing and acting
Virgo	Healing, whether of the physical vehicle or the soul
Libra	Harmonizing, through music, design or healing
Scorpio	Healing and illuminating, through pyschotherapeutic techniques or any means which shed light on the emotional patterns
Sagittarius	Teaching, particularly of life skills and spiritual values
Capricorn	Organizing and entrepreneurial, particularly good in initiating roles
Aquarius	Strategizing and speculative, often excels in mathematics, chess and music
Pisces	Sacrificial, wishes to make available to others both the personal resources and the fruits of the personal experience

With these concepts, an astrologer can point out to a client where he is going and what he is to do. Next, we will look at how to deal with the past.

Endnotes

1. The theosophical term for this aspect of being is rajassic.
2. Bear in mind here Yogananda's statement to the effect there are many holy men in India who will have to reincarnate as humble householders (ie, who have a developmental need to become more practical and materially responsible).
3. Years of practical experience have revealed to us just how powerful the Moon is, and people who have no concept of personal development are likely to be coming "off The Moon" (ie, responding to conditioning via the filter of the Moon sign and house placement rather than that of the Sun). In extreme cases, they can be living in an entirely reactive way and almost wholly out of touch with their sun sign, a fact obscured by the assumption created by popular astrology that we are all expressing our sun signs. Most certainly, this is not the case, which is the reason why pure esoteric astrology is too far in advance of where we are. Most of us still have to learn how to be and to do at the level of the personality. These lessons are taught by the Sun and Saturn. The number of aspects received by the Sun and moon, respectively, will

95

have a bearing on their relative strength as will their signs and house placements. One would not expect a poorly aspected sun in either the sign of its detriment or fall or in a cadent house to be able to give a stronger expression than a well-aspected Moon in a cardinal house and in its own sign or that of its elevation. The introduction of esoteric ideas should never be taken as an invitation to abandon conventional astrological law!

4. In this context, do not overlook Linda Goodman's excellent and widely distributed book, *Sun Signs*. It may be a mass-market book, but it is extremely insightful, as is the less well known *Love Signs*.

5. Without recognition from others, a Leo will die, spiritually, emotionally, or physically. In esotericism, death and isolation are synonyms.

6. D.K. has defined service as recognising a need and knowing how to go about meeting it. It is the intention behind it and not the form of it that will turn the contribution into service. It is equally important to recognise, however, that contribution can be made without any concept of service. People who have no spiritual inclinations are not simply wasting their time! They too are transforming energy and contributing, but with a different motivation.

Chapter 8

Inheritance: Creating the Synthesis between Past and Present

"The Moon is the symbol of the response of the dead lives to the outer spiritual impact."
—D.K.

"The only thing in your mind is what you have put there."—John de Ruiter

Inheritance

As soul consciousness establishes contact with the physical realms (see Endnote 1), through the incarnating personality, it recognises the old mental and emotional garments worn by previous personalities and uses them to kit out its new personality, but this time, they are in for a different kind of usage because the soul will have a different intention for its new personality vehicle. Every new incarnation is a blend of old and new: familiar personality characteristics and a new intention. In horoscopy, the Sun by sign and house placement holds the secret of the new intention because it is related to will; the Moon and Saturn show the old ways of thinking about self and life and are related to consciousness.

In the previous chapter, we looked at the new intention. In this chapter, we examine the legacy of the past.

Inheritance

Defines: The idea of self held in previous lifetimes
Principal tools: The Moon and Saturn
Context: The perimeter fence of the personality is found upon the mental plane. The causal body is built on the upper subplanes of the mental plane and creates a bridge between the personality and the soul that will eventually take the personality over that perimeter fence. Then, the personality can comprehend what it is doing and see the extent to which it is limiting itself. From that point, release becomes a possibility (see Endnote 2). Each new incarnation is a new opportunity to move closer to that point of realisation. Each new incarnation, as noted above, is a synthesis of old and new.

Astrological significance:

Saturn represents the idea of self, the mental/emotional preoccupation that passes on lifetime after lifetime. The Moon represents the most recent past-life identity in which the Saturnian preoccupation was blended with a new intention and new opportunities.

Considerations:

- The sign and house position of the Moon describe the quality of the consciousness (D.K.: "thinking in the heart") in past life and, to a degree, the circumstances in which that consciousness was formed.

- In giving this role to the Moon, we are not at variance with its representation in conventional astrology; we are simply taking it further. The Moon *does* describe the emotional nature because emotion exerts the most powerful influence upon the formation of consciousness up to the third initiation, and it does represent the mother because the mother provides continuity between the present incarnation and past life.

- In a natal chart, it is possible for the Moon and Saturn to be telling an entirely different story. For example, the Moon could be in Libra in the sixth house and Saturn in Aries in the twelfth house, in which case, a lifetime in which a greater capacity to understand other people and to find a role in helping others could be part of the soul's strategy to release the personality from the fear of the consequences of being assertive and self-directing (which is a characteristic of Saturn in Aries) and the sense of bleakness and purposelessness (which is characteristic of Saturn in the twelfth house).

- The soul is a consummate strategist. Do not underestimate its capacity to find a way forward for the personality no matter how exclusive Saturn has become (see Endnote 3).

- It is important to be aware that the filter of the past (the combined might of Saturn and the Moon) colours understanding and the estimation of the message of the Sun sign. An astrologer must anticipate this. For example, a client with the Moon in Cancer in the fourth house and Saturn in Taurus in the second house may take a very dim view of the astrologer's interpretation of his principal developmental requirement as represented by an Aquarian sun in the eleventh house. According to his a priori value system and perceptions, the Aquarian influence may appear to be subversive and destabilising.

- The nature of the aspect between the Moon and Saturn will indicate the extent of the "complicity" between them. Harmonious aspects, of course, will create a greater collusion.

- Do not underestimate the amount of fear involved in the idea of moving away from the values and qualities represented by the Moon, especially when these values are still the bedrock of the idea of self.

- Do not underestimate the amount of practical difficulty involved in challenging the Saturnian mindset (see Endnote 4). The mindset is stamped all the way through us like the words through seaside rock and determines the quality of our life and our thinking.

Working with this concept

There is a logic to a natal chart. By examining the placements of the Moon and Saturn, answer, initially for yourselves, why the life should be as it is—why the Sun should need to be in the sign that it is, assuming that there is an imbalance of some kind to be corrected if progress to be sustained. If you cannot find that logic by examining the relationship between the Sun, Moon, and Saturn, you will be hard pressed to give a reading that emphasises purpose. If you cannot find the logic, then the problem may well be astrological or spiritual clichés!

The difference between a sense of individuality and the idea of self is that individuality is inclusive and based upon the feeling of being empowered, whereas the idea of self is exclusive, being rooted in a sense of vulnerability.

Creating the synthesis between past and present

Reincarnation is a form of recycling: It is designed to save resources. It makes ergonomic sense for the soul to utilise what has been learned at such cost in past life. For this reason, the esoterically oriented astrologer needs to encourage his client to think about how he can integrate the quality of consciousness of past lifetimes with the developmental requirements of the present. To be able to do this, we must free ourselves from any suggestion that the idea of progress implies an indictment of what has gone before. The Western mind, which seems predisposed to think in terms of rewards and punishments, has ever emphasised the punishment aspect of karma. In fact, as a point of strict logic, there would be no point to progress from were it not for what has gone before, and that is true of individuals, generations, cultures, and even solar systems. To look at reincarnation in an emotive way is unhelpful. A client may have an emotional reaction to a description of his past-life experience, but an astrologer has no need to present the details in an emotive way.

Creating the Synthesis

Defines: The opportunity provided by each new incarnation (ie, creating balance, as its start point and looks again at the quality of the past-life experience to see what may be utilised again).
Principal tools: The Sun and the Moon, by sign and house placement.
Context: Spirituality is a process of transforming energy, and energy is transformed by meeting challenges. With each new incarnation, the familiar is challenged by the new, but once the challenge has been accepted and a new centre of consciousness has been created in the area of the life described by the house placement of the Sun, the qualities and capacities developed by past life become a valuable resource.
Astrological significance: The Sun by sign and house placement is taken as the symbol of the way forward. The spiritual benefit comes from expressing those qualities because they represent a new way of being and a way of balancing out the dominating vibrations of past life, not because there is anything inherently superior about any sign. The sign and house placement of the Moon describes the quality of consciousness developed in past life. There is nothing inherently inferior about these qualities; it is simply that the process of learning has to take a person on. The sign

and house placement of the Moon describe qualities and capacities with which a person is likely to be very familiar and express readily.

Considerations

♦ In creating this synthesis, the dominant role is given to the Sun. The qualities of the Moon are to assist, not to dominate or dictate terms. The likelihood of this happening exists in inverse proportion to the amount of consciousness present and in accordance with the relative strength of the Sun and Moon. Strength will be influenced, of course, by a variety of factors, including sign, house placement and numbers of aspects made with other planets. The techniques of conventional astrology will need to be used here.

♦ When the Moon is in the twelfth house, and to a lesser extent the eighth house, the qualities and capacities described by the Moon sign will not be experienced as familiar, nor readily accessed. In neither case will the person be unfamiliar with the qualities; it is more that he considers that they are expressed by others and not by him himself. The problem exists in the fact that the sense of identity in past life was too weak to sustain a memory of direct participation. In these cases, creating the synthesis involves looking at using the present sense of identity to recreate a conscious connection with these qualities. When this occurs, the result can be a remarkable, impersonal expression of the qualities of the Moon sign. This is why people with the Moon in the twelfth and eighth houses are frequently such effective channels for a higher level.

♦ When the Moon is closely aspected by Saturn, the expression of the qualities conferred by the sign and house placement is likely to be muted and achieved only with difficulty, but the presence of Saturn does not indicate that the Sun and moon should not, or will not, be brought into effective synthesis.

♦ When Vulcan, Uranus, and Pluto (the three planetary consciousness-changers) are in close stressful relationship with the Moon, and especially when in conjunction aspect, the developmental need to move on from the quality of consciousness described by the Moon sign is so strong that there may be a great deal of difficulty in giving expression to its qualities. This is a qualitatively different situation from that involving Saturn and one in which full conscious attention should be given to the Sun sign. The work of regeneration being undertaken by the outer planets, acting as agents for the higher self, will be following its own agenda, and the conscious mind has no control over that. But, as with the Moon in the twelfth and eighth houses, there may eventually be a remarkable, transpersonal expression of the qualities of the Moon sign, as is the case when Neptune is in close aspect to the Moon (see Endnote 5).

♦ The synthesis between the Sun and the Moon, the past and the present, has to express itself through the creative capacities of the personality (see Chapter 7, Creative Contribution).

Working with this concept

We all have a responsibility to reduce waste. Skilful use of this concept can enable a client to understand how best his resources may be used. In this matter, as with all others we have examined, beware the limitations of convention and clichés. Some blends may not be able to express themselves very readily through existing forms, and new forms/roles may need to be created. For example, we have yet to create a form that enables spiritual vision and a gift for money-making to come together in a harmonious, beneficial way. Our conditioned expectations rebel at such an idea, and we tend to require a person to be either one thing or another. Through such rigidity, we limit our potential.

Endnotes

1. D.K. insists that students of the occult recognise that the three lowest planes of our solar system (the mental, the astral, and the etheric), *all* pertain to the physical world. The purpose of this insistence is that familiarity with the expanded category will help us move on from the limitations inherent in the idea that we can know and understand only that which pertains to the dense physical world with which we engage through our five senses.

2. Release is to be understood as release from the limitations of our perceptions of our selves, not as release from physical plane existence. It is only when the idea of self has been effectively challenged and seriously weakened that the personality becomes a useful agent for the soul. In the West, under the influence of ecclesiastical Christianity, we have focused attention for too long on heaven and where we go when we die and not given enough thought to how we might, while we are still alive, bring down to Earth the Kingdom of God. This becomes possible once the limitations inherent in the idea of self have been lifted.

3. There is no such thing as an unworkable lifetime and no cause for either an astrologer or a client to express negativity when examining any natal chart. But there will certainly be many occasions when the idea of challenge is going to have to be given heavy emphasis. Not liking certain options, or not being able to recognise options, is not the same thing as having no options. In horary astrology, if the querent's question has been misunderstood by the astrologer, the appearance of Saturn in a certain place on the horary chart reveals the error. Think about the symbolism of this: It is Saturn (or rather the mindset that it describes) that makes the kinds of judgment that misunderstand and rules out options.

4. Gurdjieff, himself a Capricorn Sun, said that to go beyond the idea of yourself was like trying to jump over your own knees. The knees, as you may know, are ruled by Saturn and the sign Capricorn. To think of the idea of self as being a perimeter fence makes the situation rather less than hopeless. One can clamber over a fence or construct something to take one over. Transitional astrology serves the task of constructing the means of escape.

5. The same principle is involved in all cases: that of regeneration through extreme challenge of the past-life consciousness to reassemble it on a higher level. When Neptune is the aspecting planet, the transition is accomplished most smoothly and most sublimely. With Uranus, Pluto, and Vulcan and the eighth and twelfth houses, the old consciousness has to be

deconstructed through circumstances of extreme trauma to the personality to remove the residue of selfishness and separativeness and allow the inflowing of new, higher energy from the zodiacal sign in question. This process will be occurring at the same time as the more gradual shift in consciousness brought about by the new opportunities provided by the Sun. This should not cause the astrologer problems. One process (the Sun process) can be engaged with consciously; the other is going on beyond the control of the conscious mind and has to be experienced rather than controlled.

In this connection, we make two recommendations:

Howard Sasportas, *The Gods of Change* (Arkana)
Liz Greene, *Saturn: A New Look at an Old Devil* (Arkana)

Both writers are Jungian analysts, and their grasp of the kinds of trauma brought about by the outer planets (from the point of view of the personality and psychology) is exceptional.

Chapter 9

Soul-Personality Alignment / Conscious Decision Making

"We're living in a strange time, working for a strange goal:
We're turning flesh and body into soul."
Mike Scott
Strange Boat

"Saturn . . . is the planet which conditions primarily the point in evolution
where choice definitely becomes possible, where rejection of opportunity or its
acceptance can consciously be undertaken, and this shouldering of personal
responsibility becomes a recognised fact in a planned and ordered life."

"Saturn offers the opportunity to suffer and, through suffering, to learn to
choose rightly, to analyse correctly and to decide upon the higher values."
D.K., *Esoteric Astrology*

So far, we have made little mention of the soul and the extent to which it can be seen through a chart. The reason for this is that the horoscope is the map of the personality, which has its own agenda and it own requirements. A horoscope is always a map of the personality, no matter how evolved a person may be, and we glimpse the soul (the ego) through its window. Meeting the requirements of the personality is our first concern. Ascertaining what these requirements are has been the subject of the previous two chapters.

In this chapter, we consider what the soul requires of the personality, in addition to the general requirement that the personality become more inclusive and more responsive

The soul's role in the life of the personality is supervisory. It cannot assume this role with any consistency until the personality is sensitive enough to its vibration. Until this happens, the physical vehicle is conditioned by the stream of life, anchored in the heart. Depending upon the level of development, a stream of energy coming from the astral or mental plane (the latter is anchored in the head, the former in the solar plexus) is the point of entry for the energy of consciousness. The ascendant represents this point of entry on a chart, and the ruling planet is the principal agent, distributing to the other centres in the body. In either of these cases, the orthodox ruler of the sign on the ascendant is the ruler of the horoscope.

Once the personality is responsive to the soul, however, the ascendant marks the point of entry for soul consciousness. The esoteric ruler of the sign on the ascendant becomes the principal distributing agent, working through a network of esoteric rulerships.

Once this has happened, the personality, expressing its own goal, and soul, stating its requirements of the personality, need to start pulling together.

This becomes the state of affairs on the probationary path and is the case in the lives of all disciples. It is therefore a matter of concern for the esoterically oriented astrologer.

Later, we will look at the technique of identifying soul purpose. First, though, we will consider the matter from the point of view of alignment.

Soul-personality alignment

Defines: The common ground between the soul and the personality.
Principal tools: The esoteric ruler of the Ascendant; the Sun.
Context: The personality is a centre in its own right and has its own goal. The height of personality achievement is attained under the sign Leo, the sign of self-consciousness. Beyond this point, progress within the personality vehicle is brought about by the soul that supervises the personality. At first, the soul has repeatedly to round up the reluctant and rebellious personality, which it does through the agency of crises. Later, the personality and the soul share a goal, and there is harmony between them. Then the personality begins to demonstrate a remarkable effectiveness.
Astrological significance: This matter is examined, principally, by means of the relationship between the esoteric ruler of the ascendant and the Sun. The aspect between the Sun and the esoteric ruler of the ascendant will determine the degree of harmony between these two centres of consciousness.

Considerations

♦ The significance of the aspects between the two should not be underestimated: A conjunction indicates that alignment is in view; the sextile and trine indicate harmony; and the square, quincunx, and opposition extreme conflict. It is to be expected that this conflict will be borne out in the life in the form of crises of conscience and faith.

♦ When there is no aspect between the two, this may well indicate a very early stage in the process of picking up on the vibration of the soul. It is to be expected that the process of bringing the two centres into harmony may proceed somewhat fitfully, as transiting activity or planetary progression creates a temporary connection between the two.

♦ The respective house positions indicate areas of life that need to be brought into a cooperative relationship. The permutations here are considerable. Again, do not get caught up in clichés: The second and tenth houses, for example, may be legitimately involved.

♦ Planets that closely aspect either of the two significators may be expected to have a bearing on this matter, as would a planet in aspect to both significators, even though the two significators themselves might not be in aspect with each other (see Endnote 1). The house occupied by the "third party" would be an area of life of particular importance to the creating of cooperation between the two significators.

♦ In the case where the sign Leo is on the ascendant and the Sun is therefore the ruler of the ascendant, consider which planet is veiled by the Sun in its capacity as ruler of the ascendant and examine the relationship between that planet and the Sun.

Working with this concept: In no way difficult to use, this concept is extremely useful if confronting a client with a pattern of fluctuating commitment to spiritual disciplines or people who are torn between trying to gratify personality desires and trying to rise above them. People caught in such dilemmas will frequently consult an astrologer. It will be up to the astrologer to work out, from the chart, which will be the best ways of establishing more permanent cooperation between the two centres of consciousness. If there is no third-party planet, he will have to identify a house, using the midpoint of two significators, that can be made to supply the common ground, in which case the activities of that house and the energy centre which it represents will become the key to developing continuity (see Endnote 2). In this kind of role that involves understanding and, to a degree, manipulating energy and astrology as a discipline, is probably unsurpassed.

Conscious decision making

In a very real sense, conscious decision making represents the raison d'être of transitional astrology. Its concern is not enlightenment or any exalted state of consciousness, but rather, the cultivation of an intelligent and pro-active approach to the utilisation of the opportunities which belong to our lifetimes. The key here is conscious decision making.

Intelligent decision making opens the door of the prison created by fate. If we better understood what makes an intelligent decision, we would better withstand the difficulties involved. An intelligent decision is a mental rather than an emotional activity. Decisions rooted in emotional considerations will keep us prisoners of the past because our emotional natures are formed by past ideas of self.

Having the means to assess what is the progressive outcome in any given situation is an indispensable aid to conscious decision making. This is the role transitional astrology is able to fulfil, as it identifies the purpose of the lifetime.

Conscious decision making

Defines: The criteria for progressive decisions.
Principal tools: Saturn and the Sun.
Context: The mentality that has evolved as a result of the reincarnating process is at one time a store of invaluable experience which gives mental coherence to the separated self, and the source of all our perceived limitations. With each lifetime comes an opportunity to push out that perimeter fence a little farther in one direction or another. This slow inching forward, lifetime after lifetime, toward a more inclusive consciousness describes progress upon the path of evolution. People who

wish to make rapid progress or ensure that this is their final lifetime must try to find themselves a suitable teacher who can take them along on the fast lane. No one travels on the fast lane alone or finds himself there by accident. Those travelling the path of evolution can help themselves greatly by consciously cooperating with the process of spiritual development. What precisely is involved in this will be determined to a considerable degree by ray type and karma and will show up through the natal chart. One thing is certain, though, and that is that we will all have a need to make decisions in our lives and that each of us has the opportunity to enable those decisions to help or hinder our progress. A progressive decision is one that takes in the direction of the Sun and the area of life it identifies through the natal chart.

Astrological significance: To make conscious decisions, Saturn has to be separated from its natural ally, the Moon, and realigned with the Sun to lend knowingness and discipline to the task of breaking new ground. The house position of Saturn indicates an area of life, and the sign a way of being, which is wholly familiar. That familiarity and experience can be of enormous help in making headway in the area of life indicated by the position of the Sun. Unavoidably, Saturn is involved in all the major decisions we have to make in our lives because it controls the perceptions. In certain Eastern traditions, Saturn is described as the symbol of kama-manas, the desire mind (thinking in the heart). A progressive decision will take our lives further in the direction of the Sun, increasing the element of "manas" in the blend and reducing the influence of "kama."

Considerations:

♦ Conscious decision making involves understanding and recognising the habitual responses. To become aware that one does have habitual responses is a big step forward; to understand that the habitual response is perceived as underwriting one's existence in time and space is another major advance. This perception forms on the threshold of consciousness. It is not uncommon for a person to be able intellectually to appreciate his position, but to fail completely to understand that in the circumstances of everyday life he must stop giving this response if he wishes to get free from its limiting effects. So closely interwoven with our sense of identity is this habitual response that a person will frequently express doubt that he could break this pattern and retain his identity and ability to cope in the world (see Endnote 2).

♦ The astrologer will assess the desirable outcome by considering what a decision in any given matter could contribute to the unfolding of the potential of the chart. Sometimes a strategic approach has more to recommend it than a bullish attempt to go hole-in-one, provided the aim is not forgotten. There will be occasions when a decision has to bring about some very specific changes; there will be others when the principal benefit is not in the detail of the decision, so much as in the stand taken.

♦ Just as there may be difficulty in recognising the purpose of the present incarnation, there may be considerable difficulty in accepting the terms of a progressive decision as described by the astrologer. This is always due to conditioning and past-life memory or a fear of the consequences of taking that particular course of action.

♦ A harmonious aspect between the Sun and Saturn clearly helps the process along. The most challenging aspect is the conjunction because Saturn can obliterate the light of the Sun and destroy the will to assume a responsibility to engage personally with the process of spiritual development. The tendency will be to accept the verdict of a father figure and not to think authentically.

♦ There is usually fear involved in making a progressive decision, the fear of emotional repercussions. These consequences may be imagined, or they may be real, but either way, the content of a progressive decision exists apart from them. It has its own internal logic.

♦ Initially, a person may not feel good about a having made a progressive decision because the chances are it challenges habitual behaviour patterns. It is important to be aware of this and to encourage the client to anticipate this. We always know why we have made a progressive decision, because the process is entirely conscious, but reminders may be in order.

♦ Timing is of enormous importance in the making of progressive decisions. Transits or progressions of Uranus to Saturn create the most effective opportunities for pushing through the fears associated with the Saturnian issues. Transits or progressions of Saturn to the natal placement of Saturn produce the opportunities for courageous reassessments of the modes. Likewise, the movement of the progressing Moon through the twelfth house (see Endnote 3).

♦ A progressive decision may well upset relationships and situations of all kinds. A progressive decision is a commitment to progress in whatever form that takes in our lives. The natal chart will show this. Each of us has to decide whether that commitment to progress is unconditional. Many people cannot accept that anything that involves disappointing and upsetting others, can be progressive. On this point, there has to be acknowledgement that an astrologer cannot take people beyond his (the astrologer's) own level of understanding.

Working with this concept

To work with this concept, the astrologer has to be prepared to offer a lot of guidance and encouragement and to make assessments based upon a thorough understanding of the natal chart. It is the astrologer's job to define the rightful direction and thereby identify the criteria of a progressive decision in a given situation. The basic criteria will serve for all the major decisions of the lifetime. When using this concept, there is no place for clichés or generalisations. Undoing fate is like mastering the Rubik's cube: The sequence of moves will depend upon the start place. And keeping the spirit of progress alive and maintaining the right attitude to life is more important than a fastidious regard for detail.

An authoritative astrologer takes on considerable responsibility. He needs to be sure, not only of his subject but also of the value of offering this kind of guidance. There is no place for ambivalence. Once one departs from the lowlands of an astrology, which focuses very largely on the delineation of character, the stakes are too high. Lead from the front because you have the map, or your client may well lead you onto safer, less challenging territory where opportunities get lost.

Endnotes

1. Students familiar with the techniques of horary astrology will understand the importance of the third party, which either translates or collects the light. That idea is present here.

2. For example, a person with Saturn in Aquarius in the second house can admit that he is insecure about money, but cannot take you seriously when you propose that he take a risk and consider sharing more with other people. Quite simply, it is off his scale. Similarly, a person with Saturn in Capricorn in the sixth house will agree with you that his poor health and depressed spirits are the product of overwork but cannot seriously contemplate adopting a more relaxed attitude because his self-worth and identity depend upon his self flagellating approach to work. A person with Saturn in Libra in the seventh house will complain bitterly about how repressive and lacking in quality is his partnership but cannot contemplate making the break from the association. And so on.

3. The movement of the progressed Moon through the twelfth house brings the twenty-eight-year lunar cycle to a close. The link here with Saturn is obvious. On this subject, which, although of considerable importance in practical astrology, is not widely written about, Stephen Arroyo's fine book *Karma, Astrology, and Transformation,* published by CRCS, is to be recommended.

Part Four

Advanced Concepts

"For the aspirant and the disciple, occultism is rapidly becoming a source and system of revelation as they penetrate the wisdom of the hierarchy." *Esoteric Astrology*

"I call that man awake who, with conscious knowledge and understanding,
can perceive the deep unreasoning powers in his soul, his whole innermost
strength, desire, and weakness and knows how to reckon with himself."
Herman Hesse,
Narziss and Goldmund

In this, the concluding portion of this work, we turn our attention to the techniques that enable an astrologer to use the horoscope to gain insight into matters that have a direct bearing upon spiritual development.

In the three sections that follow, we will be doing a roundup of facts and techniques relating to rays, planets, and key points in the natal chart and indicating how these can help an astrologer gauge the level of development of his client. All astrologers must tread very carefully around this matter of level of development, especially if he has not met his client and been in his energy field. In this case, certain, crucial things cannot be ascertained with finality, and this is a major limitation that must be acknowledged.

As noted earlier, the theme of the decanates provides the astrologer with useful clues, always provided he is not too absolute. For example, the presence of the majority of planets in the third decanate of the mutable signs will indicate that the cycle of lives in which the mutable signs have been dominant is drawing toward its conclusion. It does not necessarily mean that he is ready to mount the cardinal cross. When it comes to considering the significance of the majority of planets in the third decanate of the cardinal signs, however, this may well be the case (see Endnote 1).

Before we continue, we must consider why an astrologer should need to know his client's level of development.

The level of development determines the degree of control an individual has over his personality and those problems that arise in the personality vehicle whether physical emotional or spiritual. It will affect therefore the client's capacity to understand the perspectives of an esoterically oriented astrologer and, conversely, the astrologer's capacity to understand his client's problems and preoccupations.

To a degree, this matter is regulated by the law of magnetic attraction. It is unlikely that an astrologer and client who are far apart in terms of levels of consciousness are going to muddle into each other's lives; it is unlikely that people who are on the wheel prereversal are going to choose an esoterically oriented astrologer. It is equally unlikely that an initiate will visit an astrologer of any hue in order to talk about himself. This point has been made already.

It is those who are on or approaching the path, (those who are being "reeled in" on the reversing or reversed wheel), probationers and disciples who are struggling to make sense of their lives and to use their opportunities better are most likely to consult a serious astrologer. Indeed, this work has been designed with this stage of development in mind. But even when the spectrum is reduced so significantly, the differences in focus and level of understanding are still considerable. It is the existence of these nuances that make the assessment of ray so difficult.

In other respects, however, all disciples have a common need, and that is to do what Gurdjieff describes as "come to conscience." This means developing self-understanding and eventually a sense of empowerment.

The aim of transitional astrology is to assist people to live intelligently and productively and to work with the capacities and limitations of personalities that are trying to achieve alignment. This amounts to taking a stand against fate.

Fate

If we overcome our Saturnian limitations by intelligent decision making, then it follows that we overcome fate by intelligent decision making also. Awareness of and the taking on of this kind of responsibility for self goes with a certain level of development. Certainly it is something of which every disciple should be made aware and the job of calling up this awareness may well fall to the esoterically-inclined astrologer.

By and large, those who consult astrologers and those who deal in prediction are confused in their understanding of fate. They understand that their own efforts count for something, or they would not be troubling to find out what they might do for the best, but they are unsure what their relationship with fate is or indeed as to what is fate.

Fate is to be defined as that over which we have no control. Fate is created by our personalities: It is the product of the life force meeting those aspects of our own psyche over which we do not yet have mastery.

In astrology, fate is represented by Saturn, which we described in earlier as the perimeter fence of our reality. In releasing ourselves from within its confines, we release ourselves from fate.

In *Esoteric Astrology,* D.K. says this: "Saturn . . . is the planet which conditions primarily the point in evolution where choice definitely becomes possible."

Where there is no willingness or understanding of the need to challenge self and the habitual mindset and where blame is laid outside self, there can be no resisting fate. The practising astrologer therefore needs to know what kind of awareness the client has when it comes to the matter of taking control of his own life in order to gauge his pitch, whether to emphasise control of the overall direction of the life, or to encourage the more modest goal of control in certain areas of life.

If an astrologer makes a pitch that exceeds his client's capacity to understand, then a valuable opportunity may be wasted.

We move onward, all of us, from the point at which we stand, and it is part of the astrologer's skill to be able to stand at that point for while with his client to point out features of the journey.

Endnotes

1. These observations are made in a spirit of caution for the simple reason that even after years of astrological practice and the hundreds of charts studied have not spanned all walks of life or the highest or lowest levels of consciousness in human form upon our planet at this time. The best that can be said is that these pointers appear to have validity when it comes to gauging the level of development of those approaching the path and of disciples upon the path. Such people will be drawn to the esoterically oriented astrologer. These pointers should help to prepare an astrologer in advance of talking with his client, but not to shut his mind. In the presence of the client, many things will become apparent. A person can know much at an intellectual level and understand little; conversely, a person who has no interest or awareness in concepts may have an astounding grasp on how to live productively and are no less spiritually potent for being unconcerned with theory.

Chapter 10

The Cross of the Heavens

"1. The Mutable Cross—the unrepentant thief—Humanity.
2. The Fixed Cross—the repentant thief—Hierarchy.
3. The Cardinal Cross—the Cross of Christ—Shamballa."
—D.K., *Esoteric Astrology*

Ascertaining the cross of the heavens, or the Cross of Consciousness upon which a person is developing, is the first and most basic exercise to be undertaken to gauge the stage of development. Because it is of such a highly sensitive nature, the information given here is not all there is to say on the subject, but it is sufficient to provide a useful guide (see Endnote 1).

The value of counting the number of planets in each of the cardinal, fixed, and mutable signs is recognised by conventional astrology as a means of gauging temperament. The esoteric method of assessing the cross of consciousness differs from this, and it is important to distinguish between the two.

For the purposes of this exercise, the natal chart should be recast using the equal house system, and the planets Vulcan and the Earth should be included.

As its basic structure, the cross of the heavens uses the arms of the twelve houses.

The divisions are as follows:
- The mutable cross, third, sixth, ninth, and twelfth houses
- The fixed cross, second, fifth, eighth, and eleventh houses
- The cardinal cross: first, fourth, seventh, and tenth houses.

- Any planet within those houses must be considered to lend its influence to the appropriate cross (for example, in the chart of Michael, Jupiter at eleven degrees of Pisces, is attributed to the cardinal cross because it falls in the tenth house).
- The closer the planet is to the house cusp, the stronger its influence, and the conventional method of ascertaining through which house will work influence of a planet near a cusp should be used.
- To have only two arms activated does not create a cross, but that influence should be noted.

113

♦ To have three of the four arms of the cross activated is adequate. Because of its nature, the T-cross configuration will throw a person into the empty house (see Endnote 2)

♦ The empty house must be viewed as an area of latency; development in this area during the course of the lifetime is essential if progress is to be maintained.

The signs involved must then be considered. This requires us to use the conventional understanding of the crosses. The two levels of influence are then blended.

The Qualities / Zodiacal signs	Orthodox rulers	Esoteric rulers
Mutable / Gemini, Virgo, Sagittarius, Pisces	Mercury & Jupiter	Venus, the Moon, the Earth, Pluto
Fixed / Taurus, Leo, Scorpio, Aquarius	Venus, the Sun, Mars, Saturn	Vulcan, the Sun, Mars, Jupiter
Cardinal / Aries, Cancer, Libra, Capricorn	Mars, the Moon, Venus, Saturn	Mercury, Neptune, Uranus, Saturn

Third, sixth, ninth and twelfth houses

♦ When mutable signs are involved, the experience is quintessentially that of the mutable cross (the mutable cross with a mutable overlay).

♦ The presence in these houses of the orthodox rulers of the mutable signs and, secondarily, the esoteric rulers will emphasise the mutable cross theme.

♦ The first decanate of the zodiacal signs on the cusps of the houses will also emphasise this theme. (This, of course, will be determined by the degree on the ascendant if the equal house system is used.)

♦ When the fixed or cardinal signs appear on the cusps of these houses in which the mutable planets are located, the mutable experience is being overlaid with the influence of another cross, and this may be taken as a sign that a person is moving out of the quintessentially mutable phases.

Second, fifth, eighth, and eleventh houses

♦ When the fixed signs are involved, the experience is quintessentially that of the fixed cross.

♦ The presence of the orthodox or the esoteric rulers will emphasise the fixed cross theme.

♦ The second decanate of the zodiacal signs on the house cusps will also emphasise this theme.

♦ When the mutable or cardinal signs appear on the cusps of the houses in which the planets in fixed signs are located, then the fixed cross experience is being overlaid with that of another cross.

First, fourth, seventh, and tenth houses

- ♦ When the cardinal signs are involved, the experience is quintessentially that of the cardinal cross.
- ♦ The presence of the esoteric rulers will emphasise the cardinal cross theme.
- ♦ The third decanate of the zodiacal signs on the house cusps will also emphasise this theme.
- ♦ When the mutable or fixed signs appear on the cusps of the houses in which the planets in cardinal signs are located, the cardinal cross experience is being overlaid with that of another cross.
- ♦ A T-cross of planets of any quality in these houses denotes initiation during the course of the lifetime (see below).

The following is offered as guidance only:

- ♦ The charts of people approaching the path are likely to have the mutable cross overlaid with the fixed cross.
- ♦ Those of probationers and disciples are likely to show the mutable cross overlaid with the fixed cross or the fixed cross overlaid with the mutable cross.
- ♦ Those of accepted disciples are likely to show the quintessential fixed cross (the fixed cross with a fixed overlay).
- ♦ When two arms of two different crosses are emphasised, this indicates a state of equilibrium, which is useful for the task of balancing the psyche.
- ♦ Those taking initiations of all levels will have T-crosses in cardinal houses:
  - ♦ mutable planets /cardinal houses = first initiation
  - ♦ fixed planets / cardinal houses = second initiation
  - ♦ cardinal planets/cardinal houses = third initiation

In the chart of Michael (see Figure 2):
- ♦ The cardinal cross has a mutable overlay.
- ♦ The fixed cross has a cardinal overlay.
- ♦ The mutable cross has a fixed overlay.
- ♦ The cardinal cross is activated because there are planets in the fourth, seventh (the influence of Pluto, three degrees from the cusp of the seventh house, is felt in the seventh), and tenth house.
- ♦ The fixed cross is partially activated.

The arms of the crosses provide the framework for true esoteric astrology, and in time to come, horoscopes will be built around the three crosses and the sidereal zodiac.

Endnotes

1. The cross of the heavens, when it is analysed in a certain way, provides an absolute measure of development. Such knowledge cannot be allowed to fall into the wrong hands. We request that even the basic information provided here is used with the utmost circumspection.

2. In her excellent book, *From Conflict to Co-operation: Handling Your T-Square,* published by CRCS, Tracey Marks makes this point very well.

Chapter 11

The Sun: Personality Ray and Personality Purpose Triangle
The Ascendant: Soul Ray and Soul Purpose Triangle

The Sun represents in a natal chart:

- ♦ Our true identity in this lifetime
- ♦ The central organiser of all other planets, including the ruler of the ascendant.

It indicates:

- ♦ **By house position:** The area of life upon which a person needs to focus his expression.
- ♦ **By sign:** The quality of that expression.
- ♦ **By relationship (aspect) with esoteric ruler of the ascendant:** the ease or lack of it in aligning soul and personality.
- ♦ **By relationship (aspect) with the Moon:** The ease or difficulty experienced in moving on from past-life consciousness.
- ♦ **By relationship (aspect) with Saturn:** The ease or difficulty experienced in consciously making progressive decisions.

Calculating the personality ray:

- ♦ **Probationers and disciples:** Determine the orthodox ruler of the Sun sign and ascertain for which ray this planet acts as transmitter.
- ♦ **Initiates:** Determine the orthodox ruler of the Sun sign and ascertain the ray transmitted by the decanate of the sign in which it is found.
- ♦ **In all cases:** Consider the effect of a faster-moving planet in conjunction with the planetary ruler. The faster moving planet, being nearer to the formative world, will be expressive of ray.

Calculating the personality purpose triangle (all levels of development): This triangle indicates the planets (and the houses that they occupy) that, by widening their operational base, will assist the focused expression of the personality. The emphasis of the personality purpose triangle is activity.

- ♦ First, ascertain the cross of consciousness (see Chapter 10).
- ♦ Determine the orthodox planetary ruler of the Sun's sign and the planet disposited by that planet.

- ◆ Connect these two planets to the Sun, and examine the relationship among all three.
- ◆ Obviously, the Sun in Leo has no dispositor: This emphasises the importance of the house (area of life) occupied by the Sun as the field of personality expression.
- ◆ If the ruler of the Sun sign is found in its own sign, the Sun in this particular relationship links with only one other planet, which means that there is an important exchange of energies between the Sun, the ruler of the Sun sign, and the houses involved.
- ◆ Ascertain the house(s) ruled accidentally by the Sun.

Considerations:

- ◆ What decanate does the Sun hold? Are there significant numbers of planets (excluding the Moon) in the same decanate, albeit of different signs?
  - ◆ Collectively, does their numerical weight exceed that of the planets in different decanates?
  - ◆ Does the ascendant hold the same decanate? If so, then this theme should be noted.
- ◆ Is the Sun veiling a planet? (See Chapter 2.) Consider the connection between the house occupied by this veiled planet and the house occupied by the planet that is giving a lower (unveiled) expression of the principle (for example, if the Sun veils Neptune, consider its relationship with the planet Neptune in the horoscope).

Comments:

Transitional astrology is personality centred; it is the astrology of the aligning personality. For this reason, the Sun and the message of the Sun is of paramount importance. This goes against the drift in contemporary astrology, which has been toward the ascendant and the orthodox ruler of the ascendant. While this increased interest in the ascendant and its orthodox ruler has indicated a desire to break free from the limitations of exoteric astrology, at best, it represents a halfway house and has arguably contributed to a certain loss of direction and precision among contemporary practising astrologers. We all have personalities, and most of us are caught up and suffering in the problems generated by that personality. The horoscope will always be the chart of the personality. Therefore, it is of maximum value when it is used as such. The soul, its overlord, is glimpsed through the frame of the personality. In the final analysis, the success of the lifetime depends upon achieving the task assigned to the personality; otherwise, there would be no purpose in taking on personality form and coming into incarnation. Consciously uplifting matter is one of the jobs assigned to the human kingdom.

The Ascendant

In a natal chart, the ascendant represents:
The point of interface between the personality and its informing life, the soul.

It indicates:

The sign on the ascendant and the orthodox ruler of the ascendant describe the quality of the upbringing and the focus supplied by familial conditioning.

The sign and esoteric ruler of the ascendant describe the quality of soul energy conditioning the personality.

Calculating the soul ray (see Endnote 1):

- ◆ **Probationers and disciples:** Determine the ray transmitted by the esoteric ruler of the ascendant or, if applicable, by the planet rising or on the descendant. In the case of a conjunction or stellium rising, determine which is the fastest planet.

- ◆ **Initiates**: As for probationers and disciples, but with the difference that the determinant is the planet transmitting through the decanate of the sign in which the esoteric ruler of the ascendant or rising planet is to be found (see Chapter 2).

Calculating the soul purpose triangle (all levels of development):

Through this triangle, we discover the soul's requirement of the personality. This is to be clearly distinguished from personality purpose which pertains to the level of personality. The emphasis of the soul purpose triad is consciousness rather than activity.

- ◆ First, ascertain the cross of consciousness.
- ◆ Determine the planet disposited esoterically by the esoteric ruler of the ascendant or the rising planet and create a link between these two planets and the ascendant. These planets and the houses in which they are found will indicate the areas of life through which the soul's requirement of the personality is to be fulfilled. For the purpose of this exercise, when looking at the houses, consider the quality of the experience that operating in these areas of life will bring and how this will affect consciousness, rather than the activities connected with them.
- ◆ Planets near to the ascendant or descendant are very influential in the matter of determining egoic ray and will override the importance of the ruler of the ascendant.
- ◆ If the esoteric ruler of the ascendant is found in the sign it rules esoterically, ascertain which planet transmits through the decanate in which it is placed.
- ◆ If the rising planet is found in the sign of which it is the esoteric ruler, this greatly emphasises the role of the first house and self-assertiveness in the fulfilment of the soul's requirement of the personality. This produces personalities who assume a very high profile in the affairs of their times.

Considerations:

- ◆ Are any planets common to both the personality purpose triad and the soul purpose triad? If so, the emphasis this planetary principle and this area of life (house) will be second in importance only to those of the Sun. The expression of this energy and the experience gained through its expression will be central to the incarnation, and it is vital that the Sun and this planet are made to work together (see Endnote 2).

♦ Consider the decanates involved (see above).

♦ If the rising sign is Leo, what planet does the Sun (as its esoteric ruler) veil, and what is its relationship to its lower expression?

Comments:

The ascendant provides continuity in its supervisory aspect. This is to be distinguished from continuity in its evolutionary aspect, which is represented by the Moon and Saturn. There is a tradition that states that the same sign holds the ascendant for seven incarnations. Even if this is the case, knowing of it is of no practical use to the astrologer unless the chart as a whole shows clear signs that a new cycle is either beginning or completing.

More telling is the decanate:

♦ The first decanate indicates that this energy is new at the level of personality consciousness and that it may be handled in an extreme or erratic fashion.

♦ The second decanate indicates that this energy has been experienced at the personality level in previous incarnations and that the focus now is upon refining its expression.

♦ The third decanate indicates that experience with this energy through the medium of the personality is approaching completion and that the focus is now upon giving it a high expression.

The decanate of the rising degree is not, of itself, an indication of overall level of development unless the theme is picked up by a significant number of planets.

Do not completely overlook the significance of the orthodox ruler of the ascendant. As stated, it describes the focus conferred by the conditioning received early in life from the family or those involved in the rearing. The effects of this need to be considered because it can both help and hinder a person trying to find his true identity (see Endnote 3).

Endnotes

1. There are two soul rays. Our concern is with what is properly called the egoic ray. The calculation of the Monadic ray is beyond the scope of this course, as are the astrological indications of the higher initiations (fourth initiation upward).

2. Our experience would indicate that it is frequently the case that there is at least one planet common to both triangles.

3. Esoteric tradition supports the law of opportunity, which states that each child is born into the circumstances that are right for his development. D.K. avers that this is the case, but only in respect of biology, and warns against expecting too much of the parents and their abilities to help a child's spiritual development.

Chapter 12

The Moon/Moon Complex Saturn

"As a man thinks in his heart, so he is."
—D.K., *Esoteric Healing*

"Saturn . . . is the planet which conditions primarily the point in
evolution where choice definitely becomes possible."
—D.K., *Esoteric Astrology*

The Moon and Moon Complex

In a natal chart, it represents:
The Moon represents the idea of ourselves formed in past life.

It indicates:

- By house position: The area of life that past life makes familiar to a person.
- By sign: The quality of the idea of self.
- By relationship (aspect) with sun: The extent to which the old idea of self fits or conflicts with the present, true identity; the number of aspects each receives from other planets will determine their relative strength vis-à-vis each other.
- By relationship (aspect) with Saturn (see Endnote 1).

Calculating the Moon Complex (all levels of development):

This grouping reveals the planets that energetically are bound up with the old idea of self. As it is the fastest moving of all the celestial bodies, The Moon does not make aspects—it can only receive them. It is less the case, therefore, that the old idea of self controls these energies and experiences (areas of life) that have gone into the creation of the old idea of self. This grouping increases the amount of information available to the astrologer about past life. He will then have to assess the implications of this for the expression of the present true identity.

- Determine the planet of which the Moon is the orthodox dispositor.
- Determine the planet of which Saturn is the orthodox dispositor.

- Join these planets, which in some cases, will number four, but in others, where any planet is found in the sign of which it is the orthodox ruler, will number only two or three.
- Ascertain the house(s) ruled by the Moon.

Considerations:

- Only the orthodox rulers are to be used in this exercise.
- The planets in this grouping all resonate with the vibration of past lives, and the Sun itself may be included. In this case, there is a link between the quality of the past-life expression and that of the present identity, which the astrologer should aim to uncover and explain to his client.
- If the Sun does not aspect the planet disposited by the Moon, this planetary energy and area of life may represent a means by which the old idea of self can increase its hold in the present lifetime: The fewer aspects this planet receives in general, the greater will be this likelihood.
- When the Sun and Moon are in the same sign, they will both disposit the same planet. This planet is the key to the integration of past and present. The expression of its energy through the house (area of life) in which it is found is of considerable importance in the life and an exceptional expression of this energy is to be expected.
- Which planet does the Moon veil? (See Chapter 2).
- Because the Moon represents the etheric vehicle, an examination of the Moon complex can shed valuable light upon many health problems.

Saturn

In a natal chart, it represents:

The assemblage point of consciousness over lifetimes. Saturn is 'older' than The Moon. Saturn represents a mentality that has been building over lifetimes whereas The Moon represents a relatively recent idea of self.

It indicates:

- The way a person understands life
- A repository of experience
- A mode of being and perceiving with which a person is so identified that he is not aware of its defining and excluding role
- A point of imbalance and place of limitation in consciousness

Considerations:

- Saturn is always part of the Moon complex, but the Moon stands in challenging aspect to Saturn, indicating a recent attempt to balance out the Saturnian perspective; in other cases, the Moon and Saturn are directly in league, indicating that Saturn has not received an effective, recent challenge (see Endnote 1).

♦ When Saturn and the Moon are in stressful aspect to each other, this indicates confusion in the psyche and a tendency for Saturn to "judge" the reactions and behaviour associated with the sign and house placement of the Moon. This is the root of the poor self-image that is associated in conventional astrology with a stressful aspect between the Moon and Saturn, and will play out in the relationship with the mother, who will be experienced as a hard taskmaster.

♦ The planet disposited by Saturn indicates a planetary energy and area of life that is conditioned by the Saturnian perspective in a very direct way.

♦ The relationship (aspects) that these two planets bear to the Sun will be of considerable significance in determining the ease or difficulty a person experiences in understanding his true identity. Saturn, in close conjunction to the Sun (indicating a domineering or larger-than-life father figure), may turn the lifetime and its possibilities into the scene of a perceived failure. No astrologer can afford to underestimate the existential crisis created by this placement of Saturn.

Endnote

1. In the language of the Kabbalah and the Tree of Life, to "travel from the Moon to Saturn" in the course of a lifetime is considered to be a negative state of affairs, indicating no growth. As astrologers, we should be aware of this. It is the ultimate line of least resistance to allow the Moon and Saturn to condition the life, and this is likely to be the state of affairs in the chart of a person who has individuated to some degree, but with no interest in growth or without the understanding that growth comes at the price of pain. This is what it means to be under the law of fate.

Figure 1

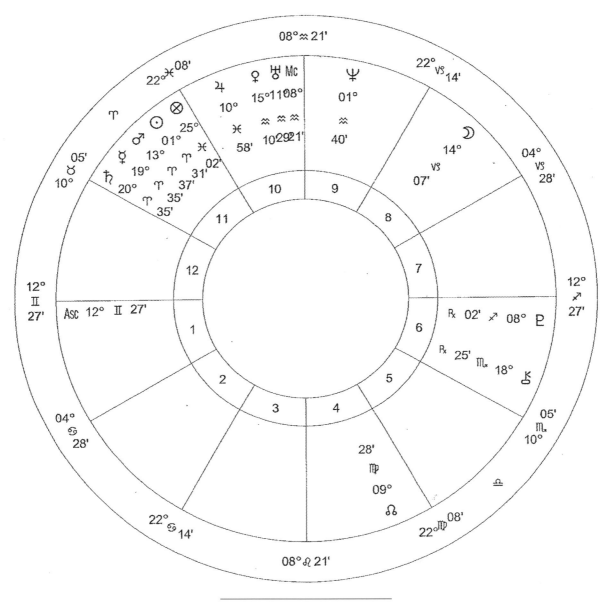

Michael 08:45
22 March 1998 50N50 0W09
Geocentric, Tropical, Koch house system
©Winstar Matrix software

Figure 2

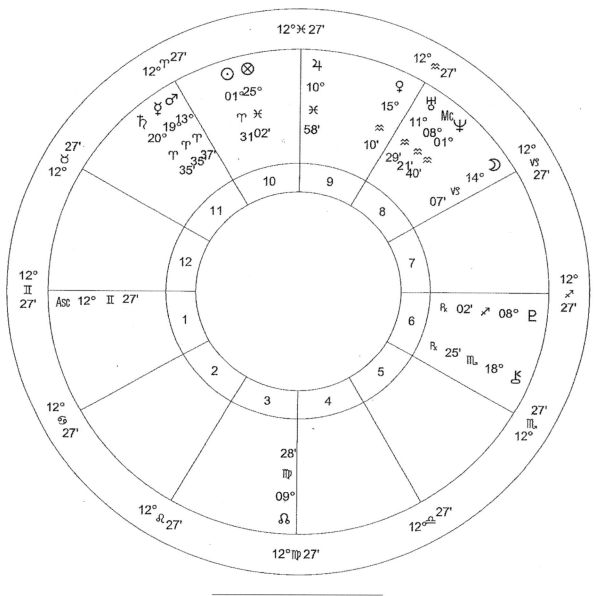

Michael, Recast natal chart
Geocentric, tropical Equal house system
©Winstar Matrix software

Figure 3

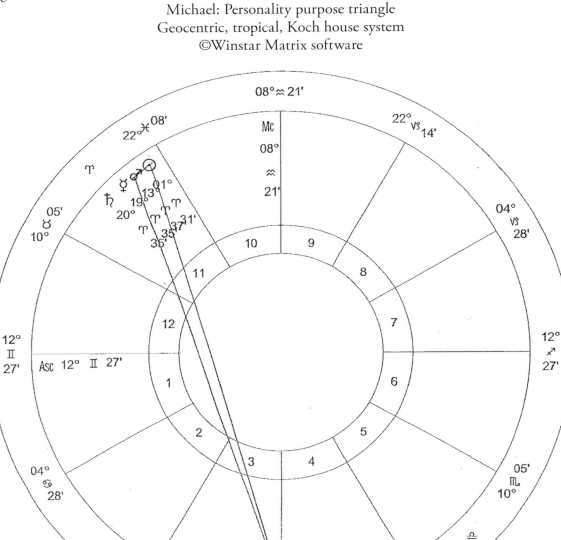

Michael: Personality purpose triangle
Geocentric, tropical, Koch house system
©Winstar Matrix software

Figure 3 Notes on ascertaining the Personality Ray

1. Establish the cross of consciousness = cardinal cross with mutable overlay. This is an indication of the possibility of achieving initiation in this lifetime.
2. Dispositor of Sun = Mars
3. Mars is overshadowed by Saturn, an agent for the third ray, which needs to be taken into account, but as Mars is the faster planet and is itself overshadowing Mercury. Mercury is the fastest moving planet in this group and therefore determines the ray = fourth ray.

Figure 4:

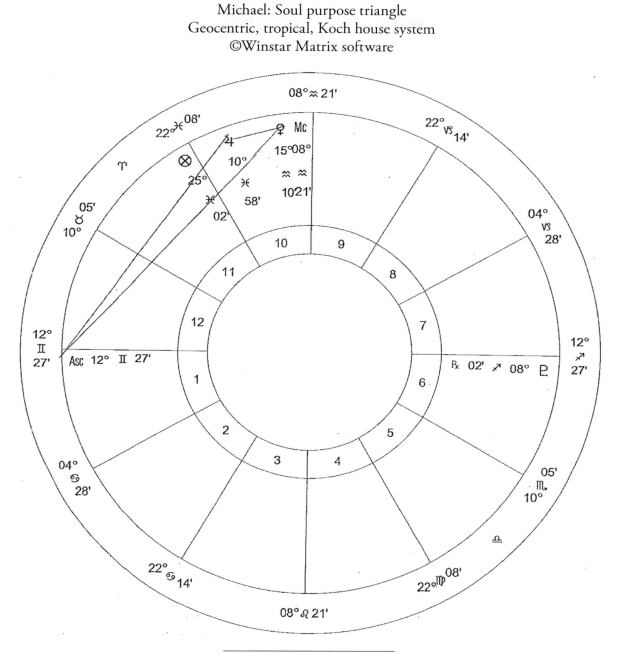

Michael: Soul purpose triangle
Geocentric, tropical, Koch house system
©Winstar Matrix software

Figure 4 / Notes on ascertaining Egoic Ray

1. Establish cross of consciousness = cardinal cross with mutable overlay. This is an indication of the possibility of achieving Initiation in this lifetime.
2. Esoteric ruler of the ascendant = Venus.
3. Yet Pluto is just three degrees away from the Descendant which is a very powerful position Therefore the egoic ray is Ray l.
4. Pluto is the esoteric ruler of Pisces, and there is therefore an important esoteric interaction between Pluto and Jupiter in House Ten, which is part of the soul purpose triangle.

Figure 5

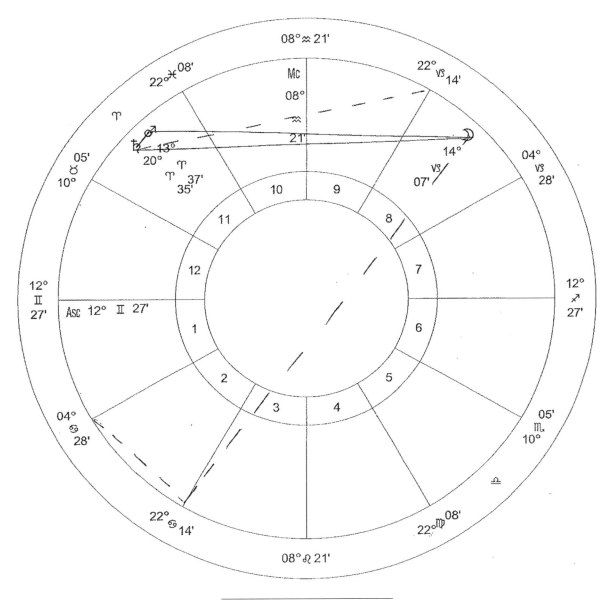

Michael: Moon complex
Geocentric, tropical, Koch house system
©Winstar Matrix software

Figure 6

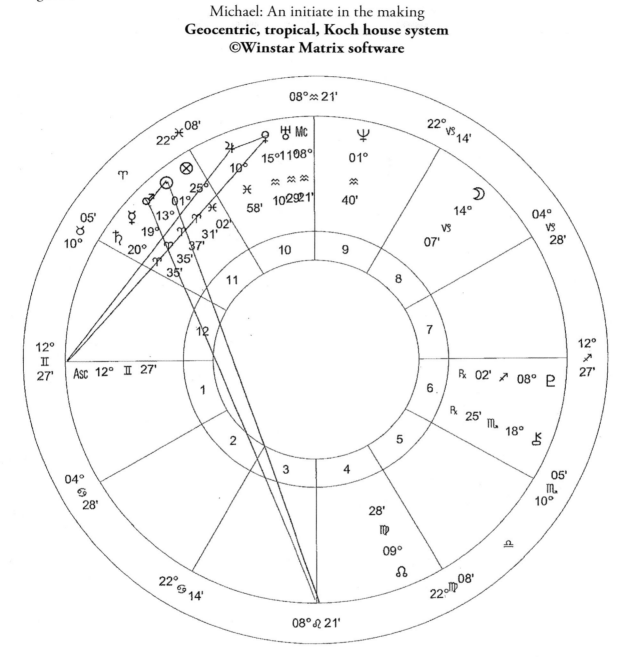

Michael: An initiate in the making
Geocentric, tropical, Koch house system
©Winstar Matrix software

Affirmation

With my perceptions, I mould the universe around me; if I would change my world, then I must change my perceptions. The familiar tells me who I am, but it is in the unknown and the untried that I will find all that I might be. My personality is my vehicle on this road, and I am learning to steer it skilfully and efficiently, cleansing the lenses of perception and respecting life where ever I meet with it, learning how to love, learning how to give, and learning how to live.